MEGAN PIUNTI

Pretty, Sexy Toaster

Finding Empowerment in Design

Contents

Art Foundations

"What do you want to do with your life?"

This is a question most of us are used to hearing, and most of us have probably changed our answer more than once. My answers have shifted from wanting to be an artist to an illustrator, briefly to a criminal sketch artist (I was really into the cop show *Castle* at the time), then to an animator, and currently an industrial designer. The common theme, which you probably noticed, is that I have always loved to draw, and I have always wanted that to be a big part of my life.

I was the "art kid" in school and proud of it. I sat in class with a sheet of loose-leaf paper and a ballpoint pen, drawing whatever I saw. The page was most often dominated by the head of the classmate sitting in front of me, depending on how interesting my surroundings were. One of my teacher's classrooms had a wall next to my desk filled with museum-worthy objects. An antique furnace and mounted animal heads were just the few that caught my eye.

For one week, every lecture in that class was devoted to recreating the wall on my blank notebook paper. Mr. Walker's economic principles faded out of focus as I narrowed in on the texture of Billy the goat's horns. I wasn't thinking too much about what I was doing or why I was doing it. It was just something that felt natural and satisfying to me. Although, the occasional smile from a classmate who noticed what I was doing definitely encouraged me.

Towards the end of the week, the class lecture stopped without me noticing. In the empty space next to my desk, I see Mr. Walker's Crocs appear (they didn't match his suspenders and cowboy hat, but something tells me fashion wasn't a primary concern for him). I look up, reluctantly waiting for my teacher to tell me I need to pay attention, or maybe even send me to the principal's office. Instead, he looks at my paper and asks, "Could I please have that when you're done?"

The next week, I walked into class to see my drawing framed on the wall, just to the right of Billy. I was happy to see he liked it so much, but also quietly irritated that my drawing of the wall was no longer accurate because it did not include the addition of the framed drawing itself. (I might be just a *bit* of a perfectionist.)

I kept drawing, and when it came time to answer that big question again, the one question that would help me choose my next steps after high school, I was nudged toward art school. The idea of being a professional painter was always romantic in my eyes, but I wanted to give myself a more concrete direction (and a more stable income, to the relief of my parents). I also didn't want to add so much pressure to something that was my escape.

So, I did my research and realized there were more art-related fields than I had thought. The reason I eventually landed on industrial design was because it checked boxes I didn't even know I had. Not only could I spend my time drawing and getting paid for it, but it also seemed like it would always be interesting. It constantly presented new challenges and new problems to solve, and most importantly, I could make a difference.

That sounds so vague to a high schooler, "make a difference," but nonetheless profound. That was all I needed, the idea that I could be doing something important and, I don't know, noble? It seemed like something I could feel good about and my parents could be proud of. I didn't stop too long to think about what "making a difference" would actually mean. I saw a few student projects online of prosthetics and assistive devices for children with missing limbs or water filtration systems for third world countries, and I was sold.

Now, I should mention that there were a lot of other fields I could have chosen where I could make a difference. I could have studied science or literature instead, and I probably would have been good at it, too. I just could not let go of drawing. Aside from the fact that I really liked it, I had this feeling that it was something I was supposed to do.

Maybe I felt that drawing made me special, and if I didn't use it in my career, I would have nothing to set me apart from everyone else. Not in the sense of being better than other people in my field, because believe me, there are plenty of people that are way better at drawing than me. Drawing made me special in the way that it makes anyone who draws special. It is unique to each person, and when someone draws something, they are adding something into the world that could not exist without them or their individual perception of reality. Drawing almost became a way of proving my existence.

There's a chance I'm just coming to this conclusion now because I'll be honest, that's pretty introspective for a sixteen-year-old who once drew a man getting slapped in the face by another man with pancakes for hands to get Gerard Way's attention on Twitter— which totally worked by the way. Ultimately, I chose design because it was the first time that I could connect the dots of doing something meaningful without a need to put drawing to the side.

After actually starting my studies in industrial design, I now think making a difference through design means improving the ways that people interact with the world. Okay, that is still super vague, but it's a jumping off point at least. This can mean improving the ergonomics of how a tool's handle fits different hands, understanding the psychology of how a person perceives the intended function of an object, and yes (what designers are mostly known for), making things *look good.*

I know that some designers really don't like the assumption that this is what we do. They might think it belittles our professions, or believe it is saying engineers do all the "real" work, and then the hipster, want-to-be artists pick the colors. That's definitely an exaggeration, but even so, what's wrong with making things look good? We are still researchers, and sometimes that research tells us what styles are appropriate for different products or what our demographic is attracted to. Aesthetics are important. Aside from making beautiful objects, we are adding value to a product, and there's something to be said for that. Also, making things look cool is fun, and that's just a fact.

Most of us (designers, I mean) are not engineers. Sometimes, there may be a little overlap in the work we do, but it is important to recognize where our own skills and strengths lay and where we should collaborate with someone else. I mention engineering because it is a huge one, but this can apply to graphic design, marketing, business, and probably a whole lot of other things. The designer is just one role in the whole process needed to make an idea into a product and bring that product to people.

A very important part of that role is visual communication. We bring an idea to life, either on paper, on a screen, or in a physical space. Maybe this idea is our own, or someone else's, or (better yet) a bit of both. Once it exists in some form, the refinement process begins, and this process cannot be done alone if it is going to be done successfully. When the refinement is done and the finished product is out of our hands, we can see how people interact with it and learn from those observations.

From my understanding, that is basically how the design process goes. At times, it can be frustrating and difficult, but that's (usually) worth it for the times that are really exciting and fun. The same basic creative process can be applied to practically anything that can be designed, which means there are so many possibilities for what you could be working on. Sometimes it could be something you're really into, like cars, shoes, or frozen waterfall climbing gear (if it's the last one, let's get coffee sometime). However, when the topic you are designing for *isn't* something you like, or even knew existed, it can still be a lot of fun doing research and making awesome visuals. Some designers might feel the need to be really passionate about the products they are creating. Others may not mind designing things out of their comfort zone because they can learn about something new and practice their skills. No matter where a designer lands on this spectrum, they can find fulfilment in their work.

During the first semester of my senior year of college, my class had a guest speaker from a company that designs healthcare products. This class was held later in the day, so he poured a bag of candy out on the table suggesting the sugar could help keep us awake for the next two hours or so. The 29 of us huddled up in a cluster of our rolling chairs, contentedly unwrapping our chocolates and trying not to think about the concept sketches due the next morning. He began his talk by asking the class, "What do you want to do with your life?"

After a beat, some of us looked around at each other thinking *well ... design.* Beyond that, most of us weren't really sure. Was that answer enough, or are we expected to have something more specific figured out by now?

It seems that the question was so easy to answer as a kid. Maybe it's because there's more pressure now, or maybe we're realizing there's so much more to it than just asking, "what do you want your job to be?"

A few people spoke up, confidently saying they want to design toys, motorcycles, or cars. The presenter nodded along before going on to show us a few different design projects he found inspiring, some from his company and some from others. These ranged from an MRI machine to an advertising campaign for Apple.

The last video was especially moving. A team of Stanford students created a solution for developing countries to help keep premature and low-birth-weight babies at a high enough temperature to stay alive. They traveled to India and worked with the organization Design That Matters to conduct research, and then make and distribute these affordable, powerful, and easy to use devices to hospitals and mothers in need. When the video ended, there was a heavy pause before our speaker broke the silence with, "I ask again, what do you want to do with your lives?"

The question hung in the air, and as I'm sure you can imagine, it hit way harder than the first time we were asked that night (maybe *ever*). I think we all felt at least a tiny bit of guilt for not standing up and yelling, "I am going to save babies in third world countries!"

What the Stanford design team did was amazing, and if I could do something like *that* with my skills, maybe I should. Is it a bad thing to want to design toys or motorcycles or cars? Is it shallow or selfish to just want a design job I enjoy that pays the bills, or can I still bring some good into the world no matter what it is I am designing?

This reminds me of the trolley problem. The trolley problem is a thought experiment about ethics. In this scenario, a trolley is heading down a track and will hit five people, killing them. You can choose to switch the track and save them, but the trolley will then hit and kill one person. It seems obvious that one person dying is less harmful than five people dying, so the switch should be pulled. This sounds like the right answer in theory, but some people might say they would probably do nothing. By pulling that switch to save the group of five people, the blood of the one person killed would be on their hands. They would rather have the five people die than intervene as to not "play God."

The question is, by doing nothing, aren't you responsible for the deaths of five people? If you have the opportunity to do something that's impactful but choose not to, do you hold any responsibility for the consequences?

Designers have the power to make meaningful change in the world, often through work that emphasizes social and environmental issues. That is a path that all design students could choose to pursue, but what if we don't? I'm only on the path of design because I drew things like Billy the goat instead of listening to economic theories in high school. I'm just the "art kid." Maybe I'm not qualified to make meaningful change as a designer, or maybe that's just an excuse to pursue something easier. If we are working at a job that is not actively making positive changes for society or for our earth, should we carry that guilt of not pulling the switch?

Intro to Design Ethics

I took an art history class titled "Design, Creativity, and Conscience" in college, which mainly dealt with environmental and social responsibility in design (those words are probably going to come up a lot in this book). It was really exciting to see all of these ways that designers and architects could make impactful, positive change in the world. We studied alternative packaging materials and methods, urban farming, minimizing waste, and many more inspiring topics. It made me feel really good about studying to be a designer. That feeling took a turn when we were assigned to read Victor Papanek's *Design for the Real World.*

I knew that this was a hugely influential book for industrial designers, but I didn't actually know what it was about. At the time I was reading it, it was nearly fifty years old. Although it was surprisingly still relevant in a lot of ways, it was a very slow read for me. (Not to mention, my studio classes were definitely taking priority at the time.) As I skimmed and highlighted, I took some notes on Papanek's thoughts on how to minimize harm to people and our planet.

Most of it seemed a bit obvious, like the idea that designing with unsafe solutions or unnecessary waste at the expense of profit are unethical practices. He also believed medical devices and design for the disabled or disadvantaged are some of the most worthwhile jobs a designer can do. I remember being surprised to see Papanek use the "r-word" when referring to people with intellectual disabilities, but I reminded myself that this was written in a completely different time.

This is easy to forget, because although many things have changed and evolved in our world, like language and lifestyles, it seemed that design really hadn't changed too much. Sure, there are tools that make it a lot easier to share ideas or create concepts digitally and the obvious technological advancements in products, but the main values and thoughts on what is considered good design or what the design process looks like have remained fairly stagnant. Is this a bad thing? Or does it just mean that design itself is such a basic human activity, to work toward improving the world we live in, that it is more resistant to change?

I was taken a bit off guard when I realized how extremely critical the author was of the design profession, claiming most things designers create are not worthwhile and ultimately just adding to landfills. I don't know if offended is the right word, but I was definitely a little upset by that idea. I'm twenty-years-old and three years deep into my journey of making the world a better place through design, and I'm just now being told that most designers are actually *bad?*

I paused and thought to myself, *maybe this is right.* Criticism is important. It ensures that we hold ourselves accountable for what we're doing in our professions. It also allows us to stay aware of our actions and their effects, which can sometimes be easily overlooked or justified when we ignore or decline this criticism.

I kept reading and got to the chapter about design education, hopeful to see what advice Papanek had for students. There was a list of learning experiences every design student should have. He focuses on the importance of identifying a problem and working with a team to both meet the client's needs and bring awareness to the issue. That all made sense, and I was a bit relieved that my classes were following that criteria pretty closely. I'm not sure why, but it suddenly felt very important to me that I could find some validation about what I was doing. Am I learning the right things? Are my intentions good? Please, Victor, give me the answers!

Suddenly much more invested than I was a page ago, I reached the end of the chapter and read, "Having experienced this kind of work, he will forever after feel a little ashamed when he designs a pretty, sexy toaster."

Wait a minute. I reread the line before realizing the author actually wrote it a second time for emphasis. "He will forever after feel a little ashamed when he designs a pretty, sexy toaster."

It took a few moments for me to process what that meant, and why I felt like my stomach just sank a bit. First of all, I paused to ask myself if I should be offended that every designer is referenced to as "he" in these hypotheticals, but again, a different time, I digress ... I knew that there were some jobs in design that were seen as more important than others, saving the world and all, but designers should feel *ashamed* if they do not fit into one of those few categories? I could understand feeling ashamed for things like using environmentally harmful materials or skipping over safety tests, something I *know* is wrong, but what harm can a toaster do? I *love* toasters! When I use my toaster in the morning for an everything bagel or avocado toast, it makes me happy.

I realize that this shame is not limited to designing toasters, but it is meant for designing any consumer product to look good. Not that they should look bad per se , but should we really be putting our efforts into something seemingly meaningless in the grand scheme of things when we could be working towards solving important problems instead? I think this is what Papanek believes designers should feel ashamed of.

When I was a college freshman, I wanted to design medical products. I think this sounded like the most fulfilling direction to me, and I thought it was good to have a goal like that for myself. In the few years that followed, none of my school projects had to do with medical products, and I still really enjoyed them. I remember thinking, *why should I limit myself to this one thing when there are so many directions I could follow?* Maybe I was mainly thinking about getting a job and what my chances were of working at a company of my dreams right away. Was I talking myself out of pursuing more noble work because I was worried about it being too difficult or failing at it? Lowering my expectations for myself so I wouldn't be disappointed (or disappoint anyone else)?

As a design student, there is this inspiring (but also very intimidating) idea that we could change lives, *save* lives, or *save the planet!* This comes a lot from both online communities and our professors. Maybe they feel that by being that driving force of encouragement for designers of the future, pushing over the dominos that could lead to life-changing products, they can maximize the amount of good they contribute to the world. Maybe they also want successful alumni to donate back to the school. Either way, of course they should be inspiring us as much as they can, but isn't it sometimes an unrealistic expectation? When most of our projects in school are things like hand tools, shower heads, or cooking utensils, should we really be that surprised to see that most of the places hiring designers are selling common objects like these?

I think these are the typical projects we do in college because they are good for skill-building and research while also working as examples of things we will probably be designing in our careers. If you don't want to design hair dryers or table lamps, that's entirely up to you. Design is a competitive field, though. If you get an amazing job offer from a home appliance company, should you turn it down and wait for the more "worthwhile" job? You might be very fulfilled with the work you do at this company if you give it a chance. If you decide you don't want to design toasters (again, entirely up to you), they will find someone else who happily will. What you have to decide for yourself is how picky you can afford to be.

When you're looking for a job, being open-minded about design directions is a good thing. Exploring your options will help you broaden your scope as a designer. When it comes time to decide whether or not to accept a job offer, you can't ignore things like the location, work environment, or salary (no matter how exciting the job sounds). You might decide to just take the job that pays the most, which is perfectly okay (as long as you check in with yourself and consider whether the work aligns with your values). There will be times in your career where you can pursue self-direction and exploration more, but there is still a lot of merit in having constraints to work within.

As a freshman and sophomore, my design projects had very strict limitations, both in what I designed and how I designed it. My classmates and I all received the same project brief outlining the requirements and schedule we were meant to follow. Research for one week, sketching for another, then rough foam models, another round of sketching, and a refined model in either wood, plastic, or higher quality foam. Each step even had a specific number tied to it (but we all knew asking for ten drawings really meant our professor expected eleven). It took some pressure off to take things one step at a time and have help with our decision making from professors and classmates.

Looking back, I understand that this part of my education was building the foundation of technical skills and holding my hand through the design thinking parts (like identifying a new problem or evaluating how a product factors into a larger system). Maybe that's why I used to think the latter was way easier than figuring out how to use the scroll saw the night before a critique.

The last project of sophomore year was exciting. We could actually choose what we were going to design (sort of). The only constraint was that it needed to be a battery-operated tool, and it needed to address an unmet problem. We could even decide the number of sketches or models we wanted to complete for each week.

I spent almost no time trying to decide what my project would be before landing on something related to golf. I was already very familiar with it, plus my dad knows more than anyone probably should about the sport, so I knew I could get good insights from talking to him.

The project ended up being a battery-operated torque wrench meant for adjusting the angle of golf club heads. The angle affects the way you hit the ball, and a single degree really makes a difference. There is a hand-powered version of this now, which can be awkward, takes too much time, and requires quite a bit of strength. I remember thinking I was so clever for designing this, asking myself *why doesn't this exist already?*

If I were to guess the answer now, I would say the current hand-powered wrench is cheap to make and consumers don't complain enough about its current state to justify creating a new product. My solution would improve function and user experience, but it's not solving anything new, so does it really need to exist? (I'll get into this more in chapter 6.)

I'm not bringing this up to ask whether or not I had a good design, but why I chose that topic. I knew how to talk about golf, and I had personal experiences to draw from. It was something I felt I could be very confident about. In terms of finding users for research, I could just ask my family, so that would save me some time and effort. Overall, I think I knew it would be an easy topic for me. I even took the easy way out of 3D modeling and printing my final prototype. I thought modeling by hand would be more difficult, and I didn't want to spend that much time in the workshop.

I was jumping ahead a bit and practicing 3D modeling on my own, so I was more than happy to show it off in critique and answer questions from other students about how I did it. Aside from saving myself time creating the model this way, I also knew it would turn out better. Instead of working to improve what I wasn't as great at, I wanted to focus on what I knew I was good at. I wanted to feel confident about my project, and by extension, about myself as a designer.

The project did end up being pretty good in the end, and I was proud of it, but I fell into a trap that I didn't realize might be a bad thing: I was designing for myself. I was the ideal user for this product, even down to the color and graphic choices I made.

Why didn't I make a medical product? I had said just months earlier that it was what I wanted to do for my career.

In my design work (and just in general, I guess), I don't want to embarrass myself by being wrong or ignorant about something. I want to make sure I have intelligent solutions and can answer any question thrown at me. One way to achieve this is to do a ton of research, but there's always the chance that you'll still miss something (You're human, and you learn from mistakes.) A safer route is to stick to designing things you already know a lot about, but this is a bad pattern to get stuck in. Your problems are not the only ones that matter, and there are a lot of really interesting design opportunities out there if you learn to look for them.

You won't improve your design skills if you never leave your comfort zone. You'll miss out on the chance to solve different problems, bring awareness to issues, and do great work. If the research is more difficult, then it's probably an issue that deserves attention. This shouldn't scare you away from approaching it. The best way to build confidence is to try new things, fail, and learn how to do better next time. Making impactful change starts with leaving that comfort zone, and it's something that every designer should be aware of, whether or not they want to believe it.

Where is this pressure to be a designer that changes the world really coming from? Is it your teachers, your parents, your peers, the internet? The most important thing to ask is whether or not it is coming from yourself. If the main reason you do not want to exclusively design things to look good is because Victor Papanek says you should be ashamed if you do, then maybe it isn't a good enough reason. Each and every designer is allowed to decide what is important to them. Maybe it's eliminating food waste in America, and maybe it's providing for your family. Both are completely valid.

You probably have more than one thing that's important to you, and that is great! The difficult part is deciding how to prioritize these things. Your personal values and the importance you assign to them should serve as your guide on holding yourself accountable for what you do as a designer, and more importantly, as a *person*.

Another thing I have noticed relating to the pressure that exists for design students is the idea that you should identify as a designer above all else. Maybe this is an easy thing to fall into when you're young and ambitious about "starting life in the real world." Especially with creative work, it can be typical to let your work define you. You are expressing a part of you, baring your soul to the world. Even if that is in the form of a spatula, it's *your* spatula. You are a creator, and you were meant to create. You have a gift to offer the world and who are you to rob the world of the manifestation of that gift: your amazing spatula design?

Okay, okay. Reel it in just a bit. It's great to have pride in your work, but sometimes it's necessary to take a step back and really listen to yourself. As a designer, being proud of your work should come from other people liking it, not just whether or not *you* like it. We should be empowering the user, not fueling our egos. I think humility is hugely important in design. We have to be willing to take criticism and learn from it. We can find fulfillment in the work we do when we see the positive effect it has on someone else. That could be literally saving someone's life, or it could be putting a huge smile on a kid's face on Christmas morning.

Designers need to be okay with handing off ownership of their work. Of course, we know that already. That's the whole point of what we're doing, to put something out into the world and hopefully have it benefit other people in some way. Sometimes, we just need the reminder that we are not creating for ourselves. We are advocates for the user. They are the ones making the design decisions, really. Our job is to interpret and translate what they want or need into something tangible. That's a great thing, but it is still a *job.*

Some people devote everything they are to their jobs and absolutely love it. Other people go home at five o'clock to spend time with loved ones or work on a passion project (or maybe binge-watch *Grey's Anatomy* with a glass of wine) with the hopes of not thinking about work at all until the morning.

How you choose to spend your time is completely up to you. There is no shame in people loving their jobs and choosing to make that a large part of their identity. I just believe that you don't need to feel guilty for prioritizing other parts of your life. Obviously, your career is going to have an impact on who you are as a person, but who you are as a person also has an impact on what you do in your career. Work-life balance will be different for everybody, but that sweet spot where you are at your best can only be found by you.

It's important to keep yourself in check when you're designing. Don't just adopt the values that someone else is projecting onto you. Establish your own values, and use that as your guide. We shouldn't feel ashamed for what we are designing because someone else says we should. That being said, we also shouldn't justify everything we do just because we don't want to feel guilty about it. Most importantly, let that idea of checking in with your values extend past your job, too, because you are so much more than a designer.

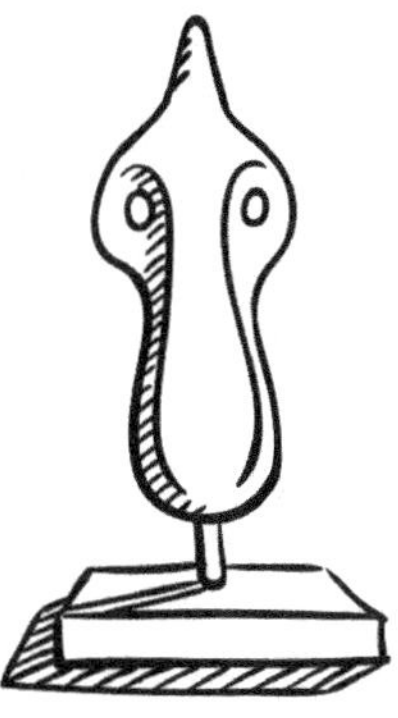

Portfolio Development

When I was in high school, the word "portfolio" had a whole different meaning to me than it does now. I saw it as the stack of drawings and paintings on my family's dining room table, which then became the larger stack of drawings and paintings stuffed into a fancy black case that would later get me into a fancy art school. I did so much online research about what colleges wanted to see, and I made a master list of what I already had versus what I still needed to create: *Self-portrait? Check. Perspective study? Check. Observational still life? I need another one of those.* For something that was supposed to be an honest expression of who I am as a person, it was largely catered to what these institutions expected.

I would lay everything out on my bedroom floor. After organizing it all nicely, I would just stare at it for a while. I was proud of what I had, but I had to make sure it was the absolute best it could be. I wanted to get into every school I applied to, and I wanted the highest scholarships I could get. My work showed a lot of skill, but was it unique enough? There was a drawing of my patch-filled jean jacket hanging over my bass amp, another drawing displaying a stack of my favorite CDs (I made sure Weezer was right on top), and possibly the edgiest of all, a *zine*. It had it all: an original poem, drawings of skeleton hands, a collage of scanned concert tickets. I wouldn't say I was particularly popular in school, but oh man did I think I was cool.

This takes us to one of the most looked-forward-to days of my high school senior year: portfolio day. This was an event where art schools from around the country set up booths at a local college and reviewed the portfolios of prospective students. I strutted in there with my fancy, black case ready to nail it. I was just exuding confidence at this point, and I was actually excited to be judged by these people that may very well decide my fate.

I went to the longest line first. It was for the most prestigious art and design school in my area, which had been bouncing around in my head as a possibility ever since I attended their summer camp when I was nine. (It had also been eagerly encouraged by most of my art teachers.)

It's finally my turn, and the woman flips through my stack of work, already onto the next piece before I can stammer out a single word about my process or intention. Then she says, "Okay, yeah, you should be accepted with this." That was it. *Excuse me,* I thought, *you're supposed to give me more feedback. And by that, I mean you're supposed to compliment me so I can feel good about myself and my work!* (I may still have some issues with needing validation.)

In retrospect, I know that's not what she was there to do. She was there to give helpful advice to students that didn't have a portfolio good enough to be accepted yet, and with the ever-growing line behind me, she didn't have time to tell me how special I am. Seventeen-year-old me, however, was not satisfied.

After visiting a few more booths from my list, each a little better than the last, I decided to see one more, just for some extra validation (I mean ... feedback).

I walked into a room with two booths, each currently busy but with no lines. I sat down next to my mom and sister, who were absolute troopers, patiently waiting around with me all day. I told them I would go to the booth that became free first so we could leave sooner. Rocky Mountain College of Art & Design was still mid-review when Milwaukee Institute of Art & Design opened up, so I went over to make my introduction. I really hit it off with the admissions counselor, and it seemed like she was *actually* interested in my work. She asked a lot of questions and made me feel like I was really seen for the first time that day. Until that moment, I don't think I realized how much I needed that.

I was always looking for praise for my skills, but it didn't mean much when I got it. I knew what I did well because I heavily studied drawing books and worked hard at those techniques. My sense of perspective was realistic, and I used a good range of values. What I didn't know, and needed to hear, was how effectively this piece communicates my unique perspective. How does it represent my personal values?

From the technical side of my portfolio, I knew what I was doing. From the conceptual side, I was a lot more insecure. A drawing book couldn't tell me how to say something with my work, that's all up to the artist.

I had some self-doubt about my portfolio. I wasn't sure if anyone would understand what I was trying to say. Or maybe they *would* understand and find it boring, uninspired, or worse yet, *basic.* (Teenage me shudders in her patch-filled jacket.)

I decided to apply to Milwaukee Art Institute of Art & Design (which quickly became "MIAD" in my head) not just because I thought I was good enough to get in, but because I felt like I would be challenged to make my work mean something.

Once I got in (with a pretty nice scholarship, I might add), I scheduled a tour with the industrial design department. As much as I was proud of my drawing and painting, I was very serious about starting a career as a designer. I remember sitting with two professors, and after talking for a while, one of them said to me, "Wherever you decide to go, you will be a good designer. But if you come here, you will be a *great* designer." Wow, did that line work on me. I know that a big part of their job is to recruit talented students, and they probably say a lot of things like this, but I like to think he meant it. I also really hope he was right.

Now that I'm finished with my degree, I can honestly say that I'm very proud of the work that I've done. Although, comparing my portfolio after graduation to the version of my portfolio that got me into college, I'm realizing what a stereotypical, self-absorbed teenager I was. I used to think a portfolio was an intimate expression of yourself. An industrial design portfolio isn't about who you are; it's about what you can do. The main purpose of a portfolio is to help you get a job. (Well, it will probably get you an interview, and who you are will get you the job, but let's focus on the first part for now.) How do you stand out from a stack of resumes, or more likely, an inbox full of portfolio site links?

If you aren't showing good technical skills right away, you probably won't get more than thirty seconds of attention. Although sketching and modeling are usually the focus, good photography and supporting graphics can go a long way when making an impression. I could go on and on about having good contrast in sketches or cool rendering techniques, but talking about that here won't do either of us much good.

The best way to develop your skills is to practice as much as you can. There are a lot of resources online to point you in the right direction, but there are no secret hacks. You have to put in the work. I'm not going to lie, raw artistic talent is a factor, and some people just have a knack for creating great visuals. If you struggle with this, you're going to have to work a little harder to be successful, and there's no shame in that! The bottom line is that people like to look at well-designed things. Your portfolio should be treated as a design project in and of itself, and if you put the same thought and care into it that you would for a physical product, the end user might just offer you a job.

If you can successfully draw somebody in, they'll want to see how you *think* as a designer. How did you go about the research? What decisions did you make throughout the process? They want to see how you developed an idea, not just how you built a thing. What you learned from testing your concept with users is way more interesting than how many hours it took for you to sand the prototype.

You don't have much time to sell yourself and your capabilities, so it's important to prioritize the most valuable parts of the project. The context surrounding what the user's pain points are or how your design will exist in the world should come way before showing off the speckled paint finish (even if it's *leManoosh* worthy, and you're super proud of it). Your problems or preferences aren't the ones that matter here. Your ability to hand over the mic to the user and create empathy for their situation is what will make your design compelling. You are the storyteller, but it's not your story.

When you can make someone care about your work, they

will be able to see more of who you are than what they would learn from your resume. What you decide to bring attention to, what you are passionate about, or what your individual creative process is can be shown in a hairbrush project just as much as a search and rescue vehicle project. It all depends on how you frame it.

You have to communicate why your design should exist and how it can improve someone's life in some way. Are you adding functionality? Does your form language create an emotional connection? You don't need to think huge, here. Sometimes, it's best to look at a larger problem, but find a small part of it that no one is looking at. Not only will it help you stand apart, but it will help raise awareness and humanize the issue at hand. And who is typically looking at your portfolio? Other creatives who might be in a position where they can affect meaningful change. (Woohoo!) Wanting to change the world through design doesn't mean you have to do everything on your own. Your role in making change can be inspiring someone else, sometimes.

As you're building your portfolio, it is important to think about what you're doing and why. This is where you can check back in with the values you established for yourself. Is this the type of work you want to be doing? If not, how can you reframe the project so it better reflects your goals as a designer? That will look different for everybody (as it should). There are so many possibilities in the world of design, so why do we see so many "ergonomic" computer mouses and "innovative" wristwatches in portfolios? (Oops, I've been guilty of both.) You don't want to look like you're checking things off a list of what you think is expected of you based on what you see from other people online. A wide range of topics and styles from one designer or artist to the next is just as important as the scope of ideas or skills shown within your own portfolio. When your work is more interesting, so are you.

While your work can definitely be a representation of yourself in some ways, it is also important to find separation between who you are and what you create. A critique on your project is not a critique on you. I have always found this difficult with art, getting very defensive if someone didn't love what I made as much as I did. Although I'm still a pretty sensitive person when it comes to my creative work (or, let's be honest, when it comes to everything), it became a lot easier to find that separation when I realized I am not creating for myself.

Product design is about providing a service to benefit someone else, not self-expression. What I want for a project isn't always what's best, and my creative decisions should (for the most part) be based on research of what is ideal for the user, while also considering the brand, the marketplace, the environment, etc.

There are a lot of constraints to industrial design, which can actually be really helpful to the creative process, even if they seem limiting . These can be things like materials and manufacturing processes or budgets and brand language. When you have constraints, you can have some decisions more easily guided, but you can also be presented with some interesting problem-solving opportunities.

A really great part about having constraints is that constructive criticism usually has solid reasoning. Someone could point out a part that wouldn't work with injection-molding or suggest the form language resembles a competitive brand too closely. Design, as a whole, is a lot less subjective than art. When you can clearly see where a critique is coming from, it's typically easier to accept it. Although, you're still probably going to hear from that one person that just "doesn't like it" and can't explain why. (Not helpful!)

There's a difference between a constructive critique and a personal opinion, but both have their own value. Art and design are both largely dependent on people's individual perceptions. What they see can determine how they feel about the object or the meaning they take away from it. Sometimes, the perception someone else has on your work can change the way you see it yourself. This can be really interesting or helpful, but it can also be annoying or disappointing.

One of the paintings in my high school portfolio was sort of a self-portrait. I didn't tell anyone else what it was, though. It was of a blue girl with an abstract jumble of triangles covering her face and creeping down her neck. Her hand is reaching out and the tips of her fingers are the only things that haven't turned completely blue yet. I'm not entirely sure what it meant. A few things inspired it, just some visuals or songs that struck a chord with me.

One of them was the song "Goner" by Twenty One Pilots, so I named the piece after that. (Don't worry, this was 2015 so it wasn't too basic to be into them yet.) I think what it may have meant to me was my expression of feeling numb, but hanging on to a small bit of hope that could fix things before they got too bad. It was just something that I wanted to make, and I was proud of how it turned out, but even now it makes me feel vulnerable.

When I showed it to my mom, I didn't tell her any of this. I just said, "what do you think of this new thing I made?" Her response was probably the last thing I expected to hear. "Looks great, but the thumb kind of looks like a penis."

Listen, I love my mom. I'm sure she didn't mean for this

comment to be offensive or upset me. In all honesty, it was a really funny (and kind of true) observation. But from that point forward, all I could think about when I looked at this painting was the penis thumb. (It didn't help that it was a blue-tinted, fleshy color, so it wasn't even a *nice* penis thumb.)

We joked about it for a while, and I would mock her throughout my first year of art school. "What do you see in this one? A vagina?" (Unless it was a Georgia O'Keefe assignment, then I guess I'd have to see where she was coming from.)

It was crazy to me how one off-handed comment completely changed the way I saw my own work. I could have gone back to change it, but it would have been really difficult to get it just right without covering a lot of what I was already so proud of. Looking back now, I'm glad I kept it that way. It's a funny memory, and the integrity of what I initially intended to create is still there in its entirety.

During my sophomore year in college, I had another experience like this. Our assignment was to design a submersible data collection instrument. The existing design sort of resembled a torpedo or some other kind of weapon, and our prompt was aimed around creating a friendlier form language to house the necessary components. This was an exciting project for my class, not because of the topic, but because we got to sculpt our designs in automotive clay (which is *very* fancy).

Before we got to that point, though, we went through stages of sketching and foam modeling. The form I ended up with was sort of inspired by an airplane, but a bit more organic, like a deep-sea fish or something. I wasn't in love with it, but sometimes you have to know when to stop messing with a design (plus, I ran out of time). The next step was to cut silhouettes of our designs out of Masonite boards, which would be used as guides mounted to the armature to sculpt the clay around. That meant there was no going back on the form you chose, which was actually kind of nice. The sculpting process was meditative in a way, and there wasn't any point in worrying about the design decisions you already made because you couldn't really change them anyway.

One night, I'm at the school working on my project, slowly packing in clay to build up the form. I remember that I should probably take some process photos, so I take out my phone. Struggling to pause my podcast and pull up the camera with greasy, clay-stained fingers, I back up to take the picture and see my form staring back at me. Actually staring. It hits me that my model looks a lot like a face. The two circular holes near the top are the eyes, the long, bulbous base hanging down is the nose, and there's even these creases that frame the holes like eyebrows. *Crap.*

My biggest mistake was not looking at my foam model from all angles before that night. The submersibles move horizontally, so that's how I evaluated it. However, our clay models were sculpted vertically, nose down (literally, in my case). In this orientation, my design didn't really fit its function, and honestly, it looked pretty dumb. There was nothing I could do about it now, though. I was only a couple of days from the critique, so I just kept going with it. If it was going to look kind of goofy, at least it could have good craftsmanship, right?

When it came time to present my project, I (unrealistically) hoped no one else would notice the face. Maybe I was just crazy? After explaining my form inspiration and surface details, one of the seniors who came to critique our work was ready to give me her feedback. She paused for a moment, probably trying to find the nicest way to point out my screw-up, and slowly said, "I see ... a face." I think everyone in the room (myself included) just silently nodded in agreement.

My professor totally understood what happened and didn't mark me down too much. I remember him saying, "This isn't a failure," even though it sort of felt like it. Although, the interesting thing was it really didn't upset me that much. The project didn't turn out great, but I learned a new skill and got a good lesson out of it. I could still be proud of that.

With my penis-thumb painting (yes, it has been forever renamed in my mind), I felt like a bad artist because the piece could not say what I wanted it to say. The message or feeling I wanted it to have was covered by something I saw as grotesque. Even though the same sort of thing happened with the face submersible, it didn't have the same effect on me. I wasn't a bad designer, I just missed the mark this time, and that was okay. I think I felt better about this piece because I was designing for an assigned function and aesthetic that came with constraints. It was something I made, but it was not an extension of myself by any means.

I think this is a big difference between art and design for myself. Art is more self-indulgent, and design is more selfless. Both have merit, and the last thing I want to do is diminish the value of art. It is still a very important part of my life, and my relationship with it will differ from anyone else's. What I want to bring attention to here is the shift in mindset I made from artist to designer.

It's difficult to compare art and design, but I'm going to take a stab at it anyway. Art and design are not in competition. They coexist and often influence each other. They are also not mutually exclusive, and there are a lot of bodies of work that walk the line between them. Artists and designers are both creators, but when they put their work into the world, they are often looking for different reactions.

An artist might want their work to be seen by as many people as possible and make those people contemplate or feel something. While some designers will have their work seen by many, too, and may even get some of the praise or fame that well-known artists find, that shouldn't be the goal. Designers should be okay with not being known for their work, and instead, they should focus on the way their work can improve someone's life, probably in a very tangible or practical way. People can benefit from good design without truly appreciating it, and that's what will happen in most cases.

Another difference is that design is often a collaborative process, so unlike a lot of art, a personal intention is not typically at the core of it. In this case, you don't have to take full responsibility, but you also don't get all of the credit. In the end, a good design team will have better results than one designer alone . If the goal is to make the best product you can, which it should be, then you should work with others to get it there.

You don't have all the answers, and building off of one another's ideas (or at least recognizing the bad ones) will almost always have better results for the user. That's way more important than being able to put only your name on it. And the truth is that most people won't even pay attention to that anyway.

I think that it boils down to this: the work of artists drives the way people think, and the way people think drives the work of designers. Although, when it comes to presenting that work in a portfolio, everyone is just trying to show how special they are, whether they want recognition, want people to hear what they have to say, or just want to get a job.

For designers, the portfolio is a tool for you to show the value that you can offer. You will probably always feel a bit critical towards it or worry about whether or not it meets expectations, but it is not a reflection of who you are. It is a reflection of the incredible things you can do, and this will continue to grow and change alongside you. As a designer, that is what you should be most proud of: your growth.

Social Media Management

Y ou're scrolling through Instagram and see beautiful photos. Some are from people you know, some you have never even met, but they all look so perfect. There's the bikini pose on a beach, the yoga poses on a mountain, the group of friends at a trendy new bar. I'm sure we all have seen these. Yet, it's important to remind ourselves that we are seeing the best of people. Not just their best angles, but their best moments. No one is posting the super crowded flight they took for their vacation or their pit stains from hiking for only an hour, or the annoying drama between friends that ruined the night. We know this, but we still see these photos, the best of the best, and think *I want my life to be like that.*

Maybe it's kind of toxic, or maybe it inspires people to get off their asses and have new, fun experiences of their own. Probably both. But why am I talking about this? Because designers do the same thing.

There is a pretty big community on Instagram for industrial designers. **#Industrialdesign** has over four million posts as I'm writing this. It's not just young people, either. There are a lot of students on there for sure, but actual design professionals are so active on the platform, too.

When my college held an industrial design conference my freshman year, I was having a conversation with a professional. (Don't give me too much credit for networking, my professor just grabbed me from the hall and asked me to show the guy to the room he was presenting in.) One of the first things he asked me was, "Do you have an Instagram for your design work?" I did, and we exchanged handles. Not business cards, Instagram handles.

This app that was half-filled with pictures of sunsets and plates of food was now a legitimate networking tool. (Which is great!) A community of successful and aspiring designers are sharing their work, promoting creativity, and supporting each other with something that is so accessible and approachable. What's not to love?

(Spoiler: there is something not to love)

Most of these designers' feeds are filled with product sketches and renders. Some are done digitally, some are with pen or marker, but they all look pretty damn cool. However, these kinds of posts are often criticized for not representing the field of industrial design honestly. *Wait, what do you mean? I want to be an industrial designer because I want to draw cool things, but that's not actually what they do?* Well, no, we *do* draw cool things, but that's only part of it (and they usually don't look exactly like this).

Most of the time, thinking through a concept means a lot of ugly doodles, figuring out which way this could attach to that, what shape the handle might be, or where the buttons might go, things like that. You (hopefully) have a lot of ideas, and your hand is struggling just to catch up to your brain. No time and no point in making it pretty. Once you evaluate all of the possibilities and figure out a direction, there are probably some dimension limitations, so you might want to start doing some CAD modeling (aka, computer-aided design or 3D modeling). Once you get some basic proportions to work off of, you might as well use that as an underlay to sketch over it digitally. That way, you don't have to spend time making sure the perspective looks right. Plus, working with layers is great, and that undo button comes in handy way too often.

You're probably going to need multiple variations, too, which might call for a few more ugly doodles or CAD modeling to work them out. Then, you get all of your concept drawings to the point where they explain what they need to, and your client doesn't really care about artsy backgrounds, so why spend the time on that? You add some notes and call them done, then you're onto the next project's ugly doodles until the client gets back to you with feedback to refine the CAD. When that's done, why make a pretty sketch of the final design when a render is more realistic and less work? (Disclaimer: Specific design processes will vary for each person and project. This is *an example* of a process, not *the only* process.)

A beautiful, hand-drawn sketch will look great in your portfolio, and those skills are definitely relevant, but it doesn't make much sense to do that kind of work in an actual design job (most of the time). That's not because designers are lazy and take the easy way out. It's just more practical and efficient to go the digital route nowadays than to slave over your pastels and Canson paper. Clients don't always have the same appreciation or patience for artistic, hand-crafted visuals that designers do.

Our job isn't to make art, it's to use art as a tool for communicating ideas. It's like you're a woodworker. You have that one really cool chisel that you *love*, but you can get way more done with the hand router, so it just stays in your tool bag most of the time. CAD modeling and digital sketching (using the hand routers) can still be really enjoyable and satisfying to do, but it's common to have that inner drive to create something by hand and have fun with it now and then. We are pushed to be creative every day for our jobs, and it can be really nice to take some time to be creative for ourselves. Now, doesn't it make sense why Instagram would be a good outlet for that? (Pull out that chisel!)

A lot of designers look at Instagram as a secondary portfolio. (I like to think of it as the portfolio's blooper reel.) Their websites and Behance pages are carefully crafted to show the meticulous and thoughtful representations of their work. Instagram, on the other hand, allows more room for experimentation. Create something, throw it out into the ether, maybe get a response from it, and then do it again. See what other people are creating, and maybe give their work a response, too. It's way more casual and interactive, so there's so much less pressure.

That doesn't mean you can't put care into it, though. Social media is an amazing tool for developing a personal brand, and you can gain a huge following just by posting some sexy sketches. (Yes, I did mean to say "sketches" in this case.)

When you have an audience, you are essentially an influencer, and what you post makes an impact on anyone who sees it. This brings us back to the criticism of Instagram's design community. Is the work shared here misleading of what a career in design is actually like?

Designers like to make sexy product sketches, and there are a lot of people that like to look at them because, frankly, they're awesome. The people who post this kind of content are not in the wrong by any means. They're doing something fun that allows their skills to be seen and appreciated by potentially thousands of people around the world. In the end, they don't really hold responsibility over the ways people interpret what they post. Although, it would definitely be helpful to try and be transparent about what they do for their jobs and what they do for themselves.

That doesn't mean every sketch needs a disclaimer that it's just for fun, but showing those ugly doodles or foam mock-ups once in a while could go a long way in representing your field and shining a light on the not-so-sexy sides of the creative process. Get some good lighting, frame the photo well, and I promise it will still be aesthetically pleasing enough for your feed.

I think there has already been a push in this direction, and this is great to see. The creative community on the app is such a positive thing, and a huge part of this is because there is a freedom to post whatever you want. There are so many resources outside of social media that can better explain what it's like to be a designer, but maybe your marker renders of a French press gets the attention of a student who had no idea what industrial design was before, who can now find those resources. I think that's a win for the design community.

It can be really exciting for a design student to find out about the huge presence of designers on social media. There's so much cool stuff, and everyone's so good, but that excitement can quickly turn to self-doubt. When the best posts are pushed to the top of your feed, you might start to think that's the standard for sketching skills, or worse, the standard to be considered a good designer.

It's so easy to compare yourself to the people on the app when there is all of this content just a tap away and available 24/7. It's addicting, because it's designed to be that way! This especially feels true when you start posting your own work and obsessively swipe down to refresh waiting for that little red heart to pop up. As if, what, that heart is telling you that you did a good job? Or that you're a good designer? How messed up is it to give strangers that much power over your own confidence?

When you try to replicate a sketching style that you like, and it doesn't turn out the same (or you only get like four likes on it), you spiral into thinking *I can't do this ... I'm never going to be as good as these guys. I'm not cut out for this.* Okay, deep breath.

Number one: just because you're not amazing at sketching right now doesn't mean you can't get really good at it with enough practice. Number two: being good at *sketching* products does not mean you are good at *designing* products, and vice versa. You can have great drawing skills but not have great concepts, and you can be a great designer but struggle with hand sketching. (*Gasp!*) Remember what I said earlier? Sketching is just a tool for communicating your ideas. It can be appreciated as an art form, but the quality of a render won't do much for actually improving lives. The *content* of it will.

I still believe that the design community on social media can be a really positive thing (and mostly is). However, it is important to have the right mindset going into it. This is a space where you can create and share. It's meant to be fun, and it should not be taken too seriously. Seeing work that is better than yours is a *good thing.* It just means you have room to grow! If you're the smartest person (or in this case, the best sketcher) in the room, then it's time to find another room, right? Creative communities are great for encouraging us to raise our own standards. This way, we can all work towards being better designers.

There's this side of social media where everyone is crafting their personal brand and showing their best selves, but there's another side of it that I haven't mentioned yet: *memes.* And let me tell you, Instagram is a gold mine for design memes. They pull you in with the lighthearted, relatable posts (like a photo of a guy wearing all black with the caption "people let guys dressed like this handle the CMF") but then they hit you hard with real issues in design (like the guy that can't decide between hitting the button that says "producing less and discouraging consumption of goods" or the button that says "making shit from melted plastic bottles.")

These meme accounts might be just as critical of the design profession as Victor Papanek was in *Design for the Real World,* but I still genuinely enjoy their content. (Sorry Vic, I have appreciation for your work, but I don't want to casually flip through it in the bathtub, you know?) Apparently, tens of thousands of other people enjoy these memes, too.

I think the difference is the community. I'm not reading a book alone, questioning why I went into this field and if I'm doomed to make crap people don't need forever. I'm looking at these posts alongside all of these other people, and I'm realizing we all have that self-doubt from time to time. It's a bit of a relief to be able to joke about it, and it's good that we're calling each other out on the bullshit, pushing ourselves to be better.

If we can recognize problems in the design world (with bonus points for doing it in a lighthearted, funny way) then we can start conversations toward actually addressing them and making change. Being a designer can kind of suck sometimes because of big problems (like appropriating different cultures for an "exotic" aesthetic) and little problems (like setting up overnight renders and waking up to "your PC ran into a problem and needs to restart.") Luckily, we're all facing these problems together, and we're all just trying our best to put some good into the world through design.

There is a tag on Instagram that's gained popularity recently called **#realdesignersship**. It surrounds the idea that industrial designers should be focusing on creating real products rather than just pretty concepts that don't actually become anything. Although I definitely interpreted this as a put-down at first, it's not meant to be. The point of it is to celebrate the work of industrial designers that make it out of that conceptual stage to exist in the world as a finished product. This doesn't mean you should feel ashamed if you post fun sketches (or memes), that's perfectly fine too. I think the point is to remind designers on social media what their goal as designers should be: making a difference, not gaining followers.

I think the only thing that bothers me about it is the word "real." Are you not a "real" designer if you haven't had a product of yours go to market? Well, some people would probably agree with that. I guess industrial design, specifically, is all about mass production. So maybe you aren't a "real" designer until you've shipped a product, but what would that make the rest of us? "Fake" designers? Posers? (I guess I'm not qualified to answer, considering I don't think I've officially joined the "real" designer group yet.)

I like to think that design is about decision making, and whether or not your design gets to exist in the real world does not take value away from it. A finalized product has to be designed with manufacturing constraints in mind, and that can definitely add value, but you don't have to actually take it through the manufacturing stage to show these considerations in a design.

If you are working at a consulting firm, the decision of whether or not a product gets to exist is often out of your hands. A great design might never see the light of day because of your client's budget cuts, shifting priorities, or so many other reasons that I couldn't even list them all. I honestly don't know that much about business, but if you're a student, I know it's hard to find a company to support you in developing a product. Also, patents are crazy expensive. These things aren't really a priority anyway since you're mostly worried about graduating and getting a job.

I'm not trying to make excuses here or devalue that final stage of shipping a product. That is such a huge achievement and deserves celebrating! I just don't love the concept of real designers and fake designers. There is definitely a sense of satisfaction in creating something physical and seeing your design at its full potential, but can we still feel fulfilled by digital and conceptual work?

During my sophomore year, I flew home to Detroit for winter break. After the holidays were over, I came back to Milwaukee a few days early to get my shit together before the semester started, and thank goodness I did. Already overwhelmed with the work I hadn't even been assigned yet, I stumbled upstairs from the Uber to my dorm. With my carry-on and my way-too-big-to-be-a-personal-item messenger bag, I see an empty spot where my laptop was *supposed* to be. It was not, and I immediately started crying. (I'll admit that I'm a bit of a baby, but it felt justified.)

I was upset about losing something so expensive, something that I felt sort of naked without because I relied on it so much, especially for my schoolwork. Then, I had a scary thought. Did I lose my work? So much of what I did was digital now, so aside from some loose sketch pages (that may or may not be lost or crumpled at the bottom of one of my bags) and a couple of half-decent prototypes, what did I still have? I'm not creating one piece of art anymore; my portfolio is a documentation of process.

Was I stupid enough to trust that my little MacBook would keep all of that documentation safe?

Thankfully, no. The most important stuff had either been emailed to my parents (thriving on that validation) or uploaded to Google Drive. I *was* stupid enough to forget my laptop in the plastic bin at TSA in Detroit, but luckily, I got it back.

Everything ended up being fine, but it made me think about my work in a different way. I felt that I was doing so much (sometimes spending over 12 hours straight at the school, or slumped over my coffee table at 2 AM, surrounded by paper prototypes with an Exact-o knife in hand), but what did I have to show for it? Practically everything I had done in my design classes had its existence in limbo because of my forgetfulness (or as my dad calls it, my "scatter-brain"). If all I had from a project was a PDF document sitting on my laptop, did it have any worth?

I recognize now that when you're a student, your work is worth something if you've learned from it. That could be anything from learning a new skill to learning from a mistake. If you're in school, your goal should be to improve your design skills in hopes that one day you can create things that exist outside of that folder on your desktop and make a difference. It's okay for your student products to help you grow as a designer and nothing else. Although, when you leave school and start working as a designer, it's likely that not everything you do is going to result in a finished product. That's okay, because this type of work is still helping you grow your skills. Although, could it be doing something else, too? Could it exist somewhere where it can be seen by others and maybe spark a new idea or inspire another designer? (Someone should make an app for that.)

I started to focus on digital work more and more during my

junior year. Model-making classes were replaced with CAD, and I only sketched by hand to work through ideas. I was proud of how my digital sketching skills had developed, and I wanted to showcase them better. When we were given time to work on a personal project, I chose to make a sketch portfolio. I already had one for hand sketches, which was an 8 ½ by 11-inch booklet stuffed with mismatched pages from random projects or exercises (the ones saved from a crumpled fate). I wanted my new-and-improved sketch portfolio to be more intentional. I wondered if I could use my design skills to make something that didn't have to have a practical use, but one that could still have meaning.

This got me thinking about the different tools we use to create things, like how sketching is a tool to create designs. Sometimes, those designs become products that are used for creating other things, like cameras for photography or chisels for woodworking. What if I focused on the beauty of the tools themselves instead of the beauty of what they were meant to create? This was sort of my nod to design sketching as an art form within itself and my recognition of product design as a small part of a larger creative process, not always the final goal of it. This was a collection of ten themed spreads starting with a short foreword I wrote and ending with a Neil Gaiman quote. I think I was so happy with how it turned out because I really enjoyed making it, not just because it showed off my skills.

The style and composition of the sketches were definitely inspired by the types of posts I saw on Instagram, but I wasn't making it for the sole purpose of getting likes. Although I did post a sketch or two and uploaded it to my website, I also had it printed out and bound as a book just for me (and one extra for my parents).

I think there's always going to be that drive to make something physical, even if it doesn't start out that way. There's something so satisfying about holding something you created in your hands. If the aliens come tomorrow and wipe out all technology, at least I have this: evidence that I was here, and that I created something.

I think this idea of creating is the main thing we should be promoting in online communities, whether that's through Instagram, YouTube, LinkedIn, or whatever else people are using at the time you're reading this. (Industrial design community on TikTok, anyone?) Gaining a following through your work can be great. It can open doors and give you a voice, but it's so important to be honest with yourself about what you're using these online platforms for.

Molding yourself into a copycat of what gets you the most likes or follows won't bring real value to your work. This is a space where you can put yourself out there creatively, so try to make it your most authentic self. Have fun with it, support other creatives in the community, and don't be afraid to show some ugly doodles.

Trend Analysis

During my sophomore year, I was invited to a "dress like another major" party. I know what you're thinking. That probably sounds like it wouldn't work, but my college only had five majors, each with a pretty distinct style. It almost became a game to guess what major someone was in just by looking at them from across the student union. Industrial designers often wore their safety glasses around as a badge of honor, illustration students had the most tattoos, and so on.

I decided to go to the party as an interior design student, who always looked like they were ready for a very important presentation. I put on my taupe mock-neck shirt and blazer, and I pulled my hair into a sleek top-knot. One of my roommates was in the interior design major, and when I came out of the bathroom, she and her friend were busy admiring the tan suede booties I had set out. (I think I nailed it.)

Most of the people at the party were in industrial design, so there were only a few people from other majors that could take advantage of the easily recognized red flannel with some Copic markers sticking out of their pocket or maybe a tape measurer clipped onto their belt loop. A lot of people elected to go the "new studio practice" route. This was my school's version of a fine art major, combining drawing, painting, sculpture, and anything else you could think to incorporate. An installation of a cinder block sitting on a pillow? Sure. A giant crochet penis? Put it on a pedestal! (I had a very nice view of this one from my dorm room across the street, and it really was quite impressive. I bet my mom would have liked it, too—*reference chapter 3.*)

Anyway, it was pretty easy to dress like a new studio practice student as long as your outfit was a little "out there." This could be mismatched patterns, statement jewelry, crazy makeup, pants that don't fit right, the possibilities really were endless. I found it interesting that the one trend that unified the NSP major was their rejection of the typical trends.

Whether or not we recognize or understand them, trends are pretty unavoidable. Why did every girl and their mother wear yoga pants and UGG boots when I was in eighth grade? Why are there so many renders right now with shadows of leaves over the product? Why did I wake up one day and see a terrazzo pattern on *everything*? Where do these trends even start, and how do they catch on? Lots of questions that I don't have the answers to, but let's take a look at them anyway.

In terms of where a trend comes from, it probably differs for each case. Maybe they start as a carefully planned choice from a company with a large following, like a major fashion brand's new collection, or maybe it's just a fluke that blows up for some reason, like fidget spinners. In terms of a trend catching on, I think the reason is simple: people like it. *Why* they like it may be a little more complicated.

We are drawn to things aesthetically, and we can't always explain why. Maybe it's the shape of an object, a sense of movement, or an interesting material that just makes an impression on us. For example, I have these two little bird statues in my apartment. They aren't even one-of-a-kind, handcrafted things or sentimental in any way. They're just from Hobby Lobby, but I liked them. I even started to decorate my whole apartment around them, making new paintings that matched their style and choosing throw pillows that matched their colors. My boyfriend's dad (who is really into antiques) gave him this amazing ancient Greek short-sword from something crazy like 1600 B. C. E., and lucky for him, the seafoam green of the rusted bronze matched the birds, so it was allowed to be on display with them.

I really can't explain why I put so much value into these $11.99 birds. They don't even do anything! I pretend to use one as a bookend, but it's so light that I really just have to balance the books upright and set it next to them, carefully removing a book and resetting everything when they fall over every now and then.

The point is, I was drawn to them. Maybe they were designed with those specific colors and materials (a painted wood body and base with skinny, wire legs and beaks) because they matched current home trends, and that's why I liked them. Maybe we're all brainwashed to like what we like because of subliminal messaging and the consumerist agenda. (The raging *Fight Club* fan in me is showing ... Oh crap, I broke the first rule.)

I would like to say that I genuinely liked the birds and made the decision to buy them without any influence from anyone else, but that would be a lie. Yes, I like them, but all of our preferences and choices have some kind of influence from the world around us. That's okay, though. It doesn't mean my birds are any less aesthetically pleasing to me or make me any less happy. The world would be so much more boring without any influence from others. We should be sharing and celebrating the things that make us happy, because they can probably make someone else happy, too!

Maybe sometimes we don't buy into trends because they make us happy, we just want to fit in with what other people are doing. Fitting in can make us happy, too, and there is something to be said for that, but it could also contradict with our happiness. I'm not here to shame anyone, believe me, but I do think it is unhealthy to make choices based solely on what other people think.

I know that it's much easier said than done. People are intimidating, and it's a good feeling to be liked and accepted, but it's important to ask ourselves what we are sacrificing for that feeling. Maybe you hate wearing uncomfortable heels at work, but all of the other women do, and you don't want to stand out. Maybe your heels make you feel really confident, and they're totally worth being a little uncomfortable for how people see you when you wear them. What other people think of us is always going to be a factor in our decisions (at least a tiny one), but we shouldn't let it outweigh what makes us happiest.

Side note: remember Bumpits? They were these little plastic hair accessories that you tucked against the crown of your head to make your hair look bigger. The infomercial played for years and basically preyed on women's insecurities, telling them their natural hair looked bad if it actually followed the shape of their head. (I'm not exaggerating, it literally started with a clip of a woman *screaming* because she was so upset with her "flat, boring hairstyle.") Looking back, Bumpits were not a good look, but at the time so many people bought these, or at least teased and pinned their hair to give it that same "bump." (Thanks to my older sister for using about twenty bobby pins to get mine to look right for Homecoming!)

But that's the thing about trends, right? They fade. So that makes you wonder, did we ever really like them, or were they just the thing to do? If they really made us happy, wouldn't they stick around longer? I guess that's not necessarily true. What makes us happy today might not next week. We're constantly growing and changing, so it makes sense that some of our tastes would, too.

So where does that leave designers? We want our products to last a while, not just get dumped when the next hottest thing comes out. Although, "planned obsolescence" is an effective business strategy: create products that won't have value in a couple of years, so you can sell the next version. (I said it was effective, not *good.*) I think it should be a goal for designers to make people's lives better, which means treating our planet nicely, not making the most profit. So how can designers help keep their products out of landfills for longer and discourage the need for a newer version?

Choose timeless over trendy. A timeless design that's based in refined, simple forms will be desirable much longer than something based on what's hot now. What's hot when you're designing a product may already be on its last legs by the time your product makes it to the market, anyway. Timeless design doesn't always seem like the obvious choice, though. If you want your product to sell, why would you ignore what people want right now? I'm not saying you should ignore trends completely, but maybe there's a way to incorporate them in a way that won't make your designs incredibly dated.

Laptops are usually very minimal and thoughtful in their design, but you can customize them with fun cases or stickers. I don't think my black, marble print case from four years ago is still cute, so I took it off. If that pattern was printed on the product itself, I would have had to carry around something that I wasn't happy with anymore, and I probably would have been more likely to replace it sooner. There are ways to make your products appealing without sacrificing their long-term value.

Look at Frank Lloyd Wright. A lot of his work is still drooled over, even if it's from a hundred years ago. Why? Because his design decisions weren't based on what people were asking for, but they were based on what he believed would support healthy and happy lifestyles. (Form follows function!) Incorporation of sunlight and natural elements made spaces comfortable and peaceful, while emphasis on community spaces in the home encouraged families to spend more time together.

Although, there are parts of his homes that aren't desirable anymore. Back then, kitchens were a place to prepare food and nothing else. Wealthier people may have rarely even gone in their kitchens if they had a personal staff. Now, people enjoy spending time in their kitchens and use them for entertaining, so they're much more important in a home. The same goes with bathrooms. Frank Lloyd Wright bathrooms were tiny because they were just meant for getting ready. Now, people want that luxurious "me-time." (Yay for wellness!)

Trends aren't just about physical objects or spaces. They're about lifestyles, too. Remember how you couldn't turn on HGTV for five minutes without hearing the phrase "open concept?" Well now, there's a huge shift in people working from home, and it's not as desirable anymore. People need spaces where they can be focused and productive, which can be difficult if you have kids playing or watching TV at an unnecessarily high volume in the same space.

Another huge lifestyle trend that has gained a lot of popularity is minimalism: the idea of living with less to have more meaningful experiences. (Sounds great!) While there is a lot to love about minimalism, I think it has definitely been overly romanticized, and a devoted minimalist lifestyle is not for everyone. If you decide you want to sell all of your stuff and live a more sustainable life, that's totally cool. If you later realize it doesn't make you happy (because maybe the stress in your life was coming from things other than your physical stuff and wearing the same clothes every day is kind of a bummer), then it's more wasteful and more expensive to replace the things you sold versus keeping them in the first place. So, don't buy that tiny home *just* yet! There's a different approach that I think makes a lot more sense: The KonMari Method.

You might have seen Marie Kondo's Netflix show or books on this method of "tidying." Personally, I'm a fan of her work, although, I can't say I follow her method to a tee; my clothes drawers do *not* stay that organized!. Her main idea is that everything in your home should make you happy. You should hold each of your possessions in your hands and decide whether or not it sparks joy. This means getting rid of clutter that no longer serves you (after you tell it "thank you," of course) and continuing to evaluate what you really want to keep when bringing new things into your home.

There has been such a positive response to this, and I think that is largely because it is so personal. There is no shaming someone in what they decide sparks joy for them, and there is no magic number of possessions that you're not allowed to exceed.

So, what does the minimalism movement mean for designers? *We design stuff, and if people don't want as much stuff, will we be out of a job?* Well, first of all, people will always want stuff, but what *kind* of stuff they want affects our work. Overall, I think minimalism is a great thing for industrial design. If the market starts to demand products that are high quality and long lasting (versus fast-fashion or flashy impulse-buy crap), then we will be encouraged to design high quality and long-lasting products. We can be really proud of our work and focus on how our products can create lasting value for someone. This could be how it looks, what it does, or how it was made. People want to feel good about the things they own, which means we can feel good about the things we help create.

Lifestyle trends like this can affect the way we design entire systems of user experience, not just physical products. Not only are these systems inspired by emerging trends, but they can also help facilitate them. With so many people moving to cities, for example, it doesn't always make sense for someone to have their own car. However, public transportation isn't always reliable or the most pleasant way to travel. Uber is born! Because it's now so easy to get a ride when you need it, more people can rely on that instead of buying a car.

Travel is another growing trend, especially with younger people who don't have a ton of money to spend on hotels. Hello, Airbnb! With so many cool, affordable places to stay, people can be encouraged to take more trips.

Although these two companies are not selling a physical product, they are still heavily designed, both in user experience and user interfaces (aka, our good friend UX UI). Now, I'm not going to pretend to be an expert on UX UI, or graphic design for that matter, but I'd like to talk about it for a minute.

UX UI design is really similar to industrial design in a lot of ways. You do your research, empathize with the user, and create an experience with sensitivities to both how your product works and what it looks like aesthetically. Is it familiar and attractive to the main demographic? Does the organization and hierarchy make sense? What makes a button *look* like a button to let me know what I'm supposed to tap? Understanding trends is so important for this!

Here's the great thing, though: you don't have to worry about whether or not it is timeless design. Apps can be updated with (virtually) no waste produced! You can keep pushing the limits of the graphics or interaction flow without worrying about waste or environmental impact because it doesn't rely on physical materials. (App designers must sleep well at night!)

The point is that trends can make your product more desirable to the user. However, desirable doesn't always mean valuable, especially in the long term. A trend might make your product cool, but does it make it *better*? (That's not always the same thing!) Are you slapping a VR feature onto your product just because you think it will sell better with it? Or worse, just because you *can*? ("Because you can" is not a good argument in design.) A lot of good design is just eliminating the things that shouldn't be there, the things that aren't adding any real value for your user. Would your shoe rack be better if it had Bluetooth? Should staplers have touch screens? (If you said yes to either of these, I'm interested to hear your argument.)

This applies to both the function and the appearance of products. That sea glass finish you saw on Instagram might be cute, but that doesn't mean it's appropriate for your product's demographic. It's okay to take inspiration from what you see online, but don't just copy and paste a trend if it doesn't make sense.

Also, don't you want your work to stand out or at least do something interesting? Where's the excitement in being a designer if everyone's work looks the same? Trends can be very useful and fun, but be careful not to get swept under the Pinterest tide.

Sustainable Strategies

D uring the summer after my sophomore year, I had my first design internship. Impressive, right? You didn't even let me finish! It was a whole *two days* a week, and it paid a generous *zero-dollars-an-hour* at a place called "Discovery World" (which sounds *very* legitimate). Okay, so maybe it wasn't that impressive as far as design internships go, but my commute was a bike ride through the park along Lake Michigan, I got to hang out with kids, and earned some college credit, so I think it was a win. Best of all, it actually turned out to be a really great learning experience.

Discovery World is a children's museum in Milwaukee that focuses on science and technology (it has an aquarium, too!). For my internship, I worked in the Kohl's Design It! Lab, which was a part of the museum that allowed kids to create different crafts to take home. Although there was a huge wall full of materials for anyone to use and create whatever they wanted, the lab also featured guided projects.

Every month there was a different educational theme, like physics or marine biology, and the interns designed projects for the kids. We were assigned different topics (for the physics month, I had marbles). We would go through an ideation, prototyping, and refinement process to create a project kit of materials and instructions. Pretty cool, huh? (It gets cooler!) Each month, we would get to help the kids (and sometimes the adults) create the projects we designed the month before. I was so fortunate to be able to see something I designed in its final form and in context with its intended users. (Hey, maybe I *have* shipped a product after all!)

For my marble project, I started by researching different physics experiments that used marbles or rolling balls. I came across something really interesting. If you had a ramp that was a constant radius, it would always take the same amount of time for a ball to reach the bottom, no matter where you started it along the ramp (something about the rate of acceleration). That meant that you could race two marbles, starting them anywhere you chose, and they would always tie, no matter what. I made some cardboard prototypes to test it out, and I even added a fun lever-based flag that would flip up when each marble reached the finish line.

After proving the concept would work, I went through a few rounds of refinement to create a final laser-cut template. So, with only a few pre-cut cardboard pieces, some hot glue, a little bit of wire, a small piece of a straw, and whatever decorating materials of your choice, you could have your very own marble racer/physics experiment! (It was a hit, if I do say so myself.)

My internship with Discovery World was a great design exercise in understanding the user. Not only did you have to design something that a kid would find interesting and fun, but you had to design it in such a way that they could assemble it themselves (with a little adult supervision if hot glue guns were involved).

There was a lot to consider. Was it too difficult for their tiny hands and limited dexterity? Were the parts intuitive enough, or could you have directions etched onto them? Maybe a separate instruction sheet? Go IKEA-style in case they can't read yet, maybe? It was a challenge, so even though my internship didn't involve complex surfacing in Solidworks, I still learned a lot.

I was proud of the things I designed there, but should I have been? After all, they were far from sustainable. None of the projects were very durable or necessary by any means. How many of them ended up forgotten or broken before a family even left the museum? Sure, we used recycled or repurposed materials when we could, but that wasn't always the case. Was I just making meaningless crap for landfills?

I think the key word here is "meaningless." No one can decide how much meaning an object has for someone else. Especially for kids, who don't know the value of something based on how much it costs or what it's made out of. They just know how fun it is, which is largely dependent on their own imaginations or perceptions. We all know that a big cardboard box can be way more entertaining to a kid than whatever came inside of it. I believe these little crafts had meaning to the kids that made them. I mean, how cool is it to have a toy that *you made?* You could even put your name on it, cover it with dragon stickers or do whatever you wanted to it because it was *yours.* Here, I believe the value is found in that sense of accomplishment for the kids (and not to mention their self-confidence).

And yet, because kids have short attention spans and parents don't usually want unnecessary clutter in their homes, most of these things probably still ended up in landfills (or, best case scenario, a recycling center) fairly soon after their creation. (Meaningful crap is still crap.) Is that okay? Were those few days or hours that the kid spent playing with their creation and showing it off to anyone that would look worth the small addition it made to all of the waste in the world? Yeah, I think so.

I know, creating waste is bad. But I also know that a cardboard ramp can make a kid's eyes light up, and a slap bracelet decorated like a sea worm can make his grandma jump with delight when it wraps around her arm like magic. If nobody made frivolous things like these in protest of contributing to unnecessary waste, those moments of joy wouldn't have happened. Do these objects need to exist? No. Are people's lives made better because of their existence? Sure, at least a little bit. Encouraging creativity for a kid (or anyone, really) is so important for their growth and well-being. Although we should be conscious of more eco-friendly ways to support this, we should also appreciate the value of creativity and exploration and be willing to sacrifice a bit for their sake.

There were still ways to be environmentally conscious during the creation of these projects. How could I arrange the different laser-cut parts to reduce the amount of wasted cardboard? Could we repurpose the leftover wire from a past project instead of ordering a different kind? This sort of thinking translates to mass-manufactured products, too, where one small change can make a big impact. You can't always convince your client to go with super eco-friendly materials because they can be expensive, but they're usually happy to cut down on the materials they're already using; it saves them money as well as reduces waste. (Win, win!) In the end, the materials a product is made from is not the main factor in whether or not it is sustainable. It's the whole manufacturing process that makes the biggest difference in its carbon footprint, especially in terms of energy usage.

Look at cotton. Cotton is an eco-friendly material, right? It's natural, biodegradable, and there were those cute commercials with Zooey Deschanel singing, "the fabric of our lives ..." with her cotton skirt billowing in the wind. So wholesome, right?

Well, farming cotton can actually be pretty demanding on the environment. It takes a massive amount of water to produce, and unless it's organic, it uses a lot of pesticides. Recently, more and more companies have pledged to transition to more sustainably sourced cotton, which is great. Although, seeing "100% cotton" written on a shirt tag instead of words you don't know how to pronounce doesn't automatically mean that it's the eco-friendlier choice.

What's the difference between eco-friendly and sustainable anyway? Well, basically, eco-friendly means that it benefits the environment in some way (like being recyclable or not using harmful chemicals). Sustainable, on the other hand, has a higher standard. It means that something does not harm future generations by using up too many resources or causing pollution. It's about sustaining resources in our environment, our societies, and our economies, because all three of these affect one another.

When we are focusing on achieving a more sustainable product, we need to look at its whole life cycle: where it comes from, how it's made, how it's marketed and sold, how it's packaged and shipped, how it's used, and where it ends up. You can buy a skateboard made from recycled straws , but if the manufacturing process takes a lot of energy, it needs to ship from overseas, or it can't be recycled again when it inevitably breaks (because straws might not be the most durable choice for a product like this), are you really making a sustainable purchasing choice? Actually, the most sustainable choice here would probably be buying a used skateboard instead. Extend the life of existing products instead of demanding for more to be created. (Yay for thrifting!)

But their website says I could help save the sea turtles! Listen, I know we all want to do our part and make good consumer choices to save the world and all. Companies know this too, which is why they will market their products as eco-friendly in any way they can in order to sell more.

People don't usually do a ton of research into every purchasing decision they make to determine the most sustainable option—frankly, who has that time? So, we rely on packaging or advertisements to guide us. The problem is that eco-friendly claims from companies are often misleading, confusing, or unregulated. Most of the time, they'll just slap some buzzwords on their products without having to back them up. Would you be more willing to buy a product that says it has a "bio-positive impact"? Well, I just made that one up.

There are so many vague claims that don't really mean anything or specific claims that focus on one attribute, but have hidden tradeoffs. Companies will work with what they have to make their products as desirable as they can be, especially when consumers make their decisions by comparing one bottle to another on the shelf next to it. *Oh, this hairspray is CFC free, that's good!* Yeah, all of them are. CFCs in aerosol cans were banned decades ago. The point is that companies will pull out all of the stops to convince you that their product is the best choice, even if it isn't by a longshot.

It can be really hard to make truly sustainable purchasing choices, but that doesn't mean you should give up on trying. There are some environment-focused certifications that you can look for like Energy Star or USDA Organic (these claims are actually backed up!). Other than that, doing a little research on the brands you regularly purchase from is always a good idea. There can be a lot of pressure to live a more sustainable lifestyle, but it's pretty impossible to be *completely* sustainable. We're human, after all.

I forget my reusable grocery bags at home, I drive a car that runs on gas, and I take hot showers. I don't think that these things make me a bad person. The most important thing for anyone is to try and celebrate where you are succeeding instead of shaming yourself for not being good enough. I'm not vegan, but I do eat way less meat than I used to (maybe two days a week right now). I use my washing machine often, but I always run it with cold water. Yes, these are small actions, and they might not be nearly as impactful as the actions large corporations have the potential to make, but they're a lot better than not making any effort at all!

If we strive for being perfect, we're going to fall short and get discouraged. If we accept that imperfection is okay, it's a lot easier to stay motivated to change our less-than-ideal habits.

So, why am I talking so much about making more sustainable choices as a consumer when I'm supposed to be focused on design? Well, I think it's important for designers' work to reflect their personal values. How can you be expected to design with more sustainable practices if you aren't mindful of them in your life? (Let's call it a "holistic" approach.)

If you want to be a more sustainable designer, the most important thing is to <u>do your freaking research</u>. You can't just *say* something will be made from melted plastic bottles and give yourself a pat on the back. Having sustainable intentions is one thing, but actually following through with them is another. How feasible is your concept? And if it can actually be made, does it take more energy to collect and transform the materials than it would to use standard materials and methods? Can you justify the higher cost for its intended user? Are there safety regulations for your product, like baby toys, for example, that might limit your possibilities for using recycled or repurposed materials?

This is all assuming you've already thought about the actual design of the product, and whether or not it should exist in the first place. Does it meet a need? Is it unique from what is already on the market? Does it add value to the user? Does it replace the need for other wasteful products? If you can't answer yes to any of these, then no amount of melted plastic bottles used will make your product a sustainable choice.

But wait, what if we don't get to decide what we design? Hey, I get it. You don't always get to call the shots, especially when you're just starting out. A client is a client, and you can't always afford to be too picky with the projects you take on or what your boss assigns you. Even if you turn down a project (let's say it's ... you guessed it ... a toaster), they'll just get someone else to do it, anyway. At that point, are you really helping the world or just hurting yourself?

Whatever projects we are working on, we can do our best to make sustainable choices. Maybe that's using less material with a slimmer shape, or it's making it so sexy and timeless that no one will want to buy another toaster as long as they live. Get creative when thinking of ways to reduce waste or add value to whatever you're assigned. Every design decision you make carries at least a little bit of power. (With a little bit of power comes a little bit of responsibility ... and it all adds up.)

I'm not going to give you a concise list on everything you need to do to be a planet-saving sustainable designer because I don't think it exists. (Believe me, I've looked.) If it's important to you to design more sustainably, there are a lot of resources out there to guide you. However, there are no black-and-white answers of what is good or bad. It's more of a balancing act of choices and tradeoffs to determine what is best (or at the very least, the lesser evil) for a specific project.

There are so many factors that play into the impact any product has on the world around it, and they're constantly changing with technological innovations and socioeconomic trends. The best we can do is to be mindful of these factors and look critically at the whole lifecycle of a product to determine where we are able to make small, positive changes.

Product(ivity) Design

When I sat down to write this chapter, I had a song stuck in my head. It was one of those annoying ones where you can only remember maybe one or two words, trying to fill in the rest, and you're just mumbling a short melody of nonsensical words over and over. *Badada all together now, badada da bada together dada ...* There's no way to search for it, and it's driving you crazy that you don't know what it is. Then I started thinking about Steve Martin, and I realized the song might be from *Cheaper by the Dozen* (the only reason I ever find myself thinking of Steve Martin).

Before I know it, I'm flipping back and forth from the movie's IMDb page to YouTube, playing the songs from the soundtrack. Then, I found it! "People (Come Together)" by Len. (The part I was thinking of was actually sampled from a sixties song called "Reach out of the Darkness" by Friend & Lover.) After my lengthy internet-search detour, I could finally fill in the rest of the words (which I would like to add here but probably shouldn't for copyright reasons). I felt *very* accomplished before realizing that this was not at all what I sat down to do, and I hadn't really accomplished anything.

Why is it so hard to be productive sometimes? We can have all the time in the world and still convince ourselves there is something else we should be doing instead of the task at hand. It's not just when there's something we *have* to do, either. It's even when there's something we *want* to do!

Maybe if we're procrastinating something we want to do, it's because we've set high expectations for ourselves, and we're nervous about it not going the way we imagined. This is especially true if it's a creative task, and you're second-guessing your capabilities. In this case, it's easy and incredibly tempting to use the excuse "I'm not *inspired!*" No one can really argue with that because it's an internal thing. It's like writer's block, which is never really limited to just writing. You can feel creatively blocked for a lot of things (like art and design, for example), but more often than not, the best way to deal with it is to just do *something.* Even if it's crap, it's a starting point and something to work with. Maybe it will lead to better things! At the very least, it can help you figure out what *not* to do.

There's a lot of pressure for creatives to produce good content all of the time, but it's important to recognize the crappy attempts as a necessary part of the process. It can be discouraging to work through, but it's a hell of a lot better than doing nothing (paralyzed with self-doubt and all). Although, doing nothing for a little while can also help reset ourselves and avoid burnout (emphasis on "a little"). I can't stress how valuable these breaks have been for myself. The thing about breaks, though, is they have to have an end where you eventually get back to work. Otherwise, you're just talking yourself into giving up.

Ask yourself why you're taking a break. Do you feel like you need to gain some perspective, or is the thought of working on it at all just too intimidating? You have to keep yourself on a track for the things you want to accomplish because no one else will do it for you. If you realize that what you've been working to accomplish isn't something you actually want, however, maybe a permanent break isn't the worst thing.

It's a great habit to set personal standards and make goals for yourself, both short-term and long-term. The fulfillment you can find in creating or learning something new can be so valuable, but it's important to focus on what creates value for *yourself*. Would starting a podcast really be beneficial to you, or do you just want to add another achievement to your resume? The design world feels so competitive sometimes, and I can definitely understand the desire to set yourself apart, but I promise that no one is tallying up your achievements to determine how good of a designer you are. Your worth as a designer is shown through the quality of your work (not the quantity), and it will be interpreted differently by anyone who sees your portfolio. What's really intriguing to one person might be boring to the next. You can't control that. What you *can* control is the value you see in your own work.

Are you happier when you're learning new skills, or would you rather spend the time improving a skill you already have? More importantly, how much of your time do you want to spend working on skills at all? As a creative, it's common to find yourself centering your life around what you create.

I'll let you in on a secret. Your work doesn't have to be your whole life for it to be worth something. Creative work can actually really benefit from taking time for yourself, whether that's caring for your mental health or having new experiences to draw inspiration from.

You can give yourself permission to take time off. If that's easier said than done for you, then this is me giving you permission, right now. (If you've read this far in my book, then I'm hoping you trust me enough to give me that authority.)

You don't have to be productive one hundred percent of the time. In fact, you really shouldn't if you want your work to be interesting or worthwhile. Everyone has their own balance to find between the grind and the rest of their life. That balance starts with setting goals that make sense for *you*, which means choosing to pursue things that you actually care about, that you are intrinsically motivated to work towards, and that you are willing to make some sacrifices for. *These* should be your guidelines, not what you think will make you look more impressive to others.

The problem with setting long-term goals (even the ones you really care about) is that they can be filled with a lot of short-term tasks that you just don't want to do. Those can be the easiest to procrastinate, and they make it a lot harder to be productive. Even if it's for something you're totally motivated to achieve, like getting a college degree, for example, all you care about in the moment is how boring the assignment is or how mentally draining it is to study for the test.

It can be hard to remember how important that big-picture goal is when there's a page-long to-do list towering over you. There's this lapse in motivation that can set you back, but there's probably also a lot of fear at the root of it. Is it fear of failing? Fear of embarrassing yourself? Fear of getting your fingers cut off? (Yes, you read that last one correctly.)

My college had a 3D lab filled with big, scary machines that everyone was required to use, even if your usual body of work was completely 2D. Freshman year, we all had a class where we had to build a wooden box as a training exercise. That meant using the jointer, planer, table saw, and miter saw. If you were nervous, the lab technicians were always nice and helpful. The industrial design students, however, had to get very comfortable with these machines and plenty of others. We had so many assignments in prototyping and model making that we couldn't always afford to wait for someone else to come help us.

There was also this sense of having to prove yourself. If you weren't cut out to use the band saw by yourself, then maybe you weren't cut out for design (which is totally not true, by the way). Either way, this was a big mental hurdle for myself.

It's not like I had never used power tools before. I was actually pretty comfortable with the things I had experience with. It was trying new machines for the first time that freaked me out. I knew that once I gave it a try and saw that it really wasn't so scary, it would be fine. (It would usually leave me with a surprisingly great feeling, actually.)

Towards the end of my freshman year, one of my classes was working on this huge collaborative mural that included plywood panels cut into all of these funky shapes. I remember being paired to work with a guy I had a crush on (and definitely wanted to impress). Somehow, I had the confidence to take charge with the jigsaw while he held the panel steady. No one lost any fingers! Needless to say, I was feeling very good about myself. However, these experiences of trying something scary and having everything end up okay still didn't make it easier much when I was mustering up the courage to try a new tool or machine that first time. I just couldn't get it through my head for some reason, which led to a lot of unnecessary stress.

One of my introductory projects for sophomore year of industrial design was the Two-Cut Project. The end result was a simple wooden sculpture with a unique, curvy shape and a glossy paint finish. Starting with a rectangular block, you would cut a big curve down the middle of it, repeat this on the other side, then rearrange the four pieces to make an abstract form without wasting any material. Sort of cool, but the whole project felt a lot like busy-work. I mean, was this really teaching us about design? What was practical or useful about an abstract sculpture? (And most importantly, *how were we supposed to save the world with this?*)

We were all ambitious about coming up with great products, but had to spend weeks refining simple curves that didn't mean anything (or *feel like* they meant anything, anyway). There were so many rounds of miniature models (cutting and gluing and sanding and painting and sanding and painting...) before we could even start our final shapes. For something kind of silly-looking and simple, it could definitely be overwhelming.

I remember being so stressed about starting that final model. I wasn't very comfortable with most of the machines, especially because I'm only five foot one. The miter saw handle was literally above my head, and I could barely wrap my hand around it securely. Do you ever get so anxious about doing something that you decide to ignore it as long as you can, making it so much worse for yourself than just getting it over with? That was me more often than I'd like to admit.

When I was talking about it one night to my friend (who would later be my boyfriend—and not Jigsaw guy by the way), I realized there was something even scarier to me than the miter saw. After all, I had managed to use it before. What was so stressful about it this time? Well, the material we were provided (which we needed to cut down and glue up into a solid block) were these huge planks of two-inch-thick wood stacked on a shelf. I had to carry it from the shelf to the miter saw, maybe around a thirty-foot distance. I was too worried that I wouldn't be able to do it myself and be embarrassed, or I would have to ask someone for help and be embarrassed. The thought of embarrassing myself was scarier to me than the thought of hurting myself with the saw. Maybe that's because it seemed more likely to happen, or I just cared way too much about what other people thought of me.

My friend (who happens to be six foot ten) offered to go over to the lab to help me and we got it done in less than twenty minutes. He just scooped up the plank like it was nothing! When I finished with the saw, I remember him asking, "Wait, that was it?" My mood was drastically better, and I felt like a weight had been lifted (metaphorically, I mean). Just like the huge plank of wood, the weight was a lot easier to lift with someone else's help. I had put way too much pressure on "proving" myself, when I'm sure anyone in my class would have been more than happy to help me if I asked, or wouldn't have thought any less of me if I was struggling to do it on my own. Being productive can be a lot more difficult when you keep those mental barriers up and refuse to step out of your comfort zone.

I think that was the point of the Two-Cut Project: helping us test the limits of our comfort zone. It also tested our dedication to the industrial design program. It was pretty difficult to devote weeks of work on these silly sculptures if you didn't trust that it would help you in the long run.

We spent long nights sanding our models to perfection (or as close as we could get) when we could have been hanging out with our friends or watching Netflix in bed. And what did we get out of it? Weird looking sculptures that no one wanted? (We couldn't even pick our own colors, and I got assigned a toxic sort of green.) Well, we also improved our model making skills, got more familiar with the 3D lab, and experienced working within a tight deadline. (I guess busy work can have a point, too.) We all put a ton of time into these things, which came with a huge sense of accomplishment.

That pretty much sums up my sophomore year. You devoted a crazy amount of time and effort so you could ride this wave of *I can't believe I did that!* for the rest of your college career. It might have been effective, but I can't say it was particularly healthy for the students.

Our projects were incredibly time consuming, and our professors expected us to put them at the top of our priority lists. I mean, we were at this school to learn how to be designers, right? What could be more important to us than building a six-foot-long, weight-bearing bridge from paper strips during finals week? Or sculpting form-study foam models over Thanksgiving break? In all fairness, it was definitely possible to power through projects early if you had something important in your personal life, it was just very difficult.

I remember meeting my family in Grand Rapids for a birthday celebration (both of my sisters and I shared a birthday weekend) when I had about twenty sketch concepts due that Monday. After putting most of the work off until the day before, I took a ferry across Lake Michigan to get back to Milwaukee, struggling to sketch cleanly on a rocking boat. Though, that was better than fighting the drowsiness of motion-sickness medicine with a Red Bull to finish the final concepts once I got back. I took a much more proactive approach with my schoolwork after that.

Time management can be really difficult, but it's a skill we all got a lot better at by the end of sophomore year. Although, there was something strangely empowering about those caffeine-fueled late nights. I think it reminded us that we really cared about what we were studying, and that's not something everyone can confidently say. Maybe that goes back to the idea of proving yourself to your classmates. It became this weird competition of who got the least amount of sleep the night before a critique, as if that says something about your worth as a designer.

Now, I want to make this clear. Starving your body of what it needs is not cool, pulling all-nighters does not make you a badass, and putting your health at risk is not impressive (and it sure as hell does not make you better than anyone else). I get that pulling all-nighters is necessary sometimes, and that's fine, but it's not something to brag about. If you devoted an extra hour to your project every day the week leading up to your critique, you would have been able to get a full night of sleep and still could have done the same amount of work. Although, that doesn't always work out. Sometimes, we can think we're totally on top of things until something falls through.

The very first design project of my sophomore year was dubbed the "shelter project." In teams of three, we designed and built disaster relief shelters from limited amounts of cardboard and corrugated plastic sheets. We started creating concepts individually, and when we were assigned our teammates, we presented our concepts to the class before moving forward with one of them. I was happy with what I had to present, but my professor pointed to a small thumbnail sketch on one of my ideation pages and said, "No, *that's* the one." I listened to him (equal parts of trusting his expertise and wanting to get a good grade) and worked so hard to perfect that concept and create a working scale model for the next critique. Its plastic roof was in sections that would each pivot up at the pull of a string for better airflow ... in a *cardboard* shelter. (Yeah, I was quite the innovative thinker.)

Whether or not it was a good idea, my professor told me to do it, and that's what mattered. I confidently presented my new-and-improved model at our next class, flooded with confidence from the oohs and aahs of my classmates as I demonstrated the moving panels. My professor politely waited for everyone to finish giving feedback before strictly stating, "No articulation."

I'm sorry, what? That's what this whole concept is: an articulating roof. Which *you* told me to do! Either he honestly misunderstood the thumbnail sketch, or he was messing with me to give me an extra challenge (and an anecdote to use in interviews or put into a book). I nodded along at all of the changes he recommended, trying really hard to look like I definitely wasn't holding back tears. (I'm still not sure if I pulled this off or if my classmates were just polite enough to pretend that I did.)

If my group was going to stay on schedule, we had to be ready to start building the next day. That meant having all of the layouts and dimensions finalized. Based on what my professor said, I had to completely change mine instead of just choosing another one of our group's concepts. I still had another class that night, which was across town at a different campus, and I really couldn't skip.

Throughout the class, I felt sure that I was going to completely fail the project and disappoint my teammates. I knew that wasn't an option, though. I couldn't just give up on the first project. Where was the confidence I had just that morning? I knew it wasn't going to be easy, but did I ever expect it to be?

Mentally preparing myself for the long night ahead, my not-yet-boyfriend picked me up from class on his moped scooter. (The moped was a very brief phase of his, but I'm thankful for it.) I had had a very crappy and tiring day, but feeling like I was in The Lizzie McGuire Movie riding through the streets of Rome re-energized me to get to work. I don't know if there's anything more encouraging than embodying the fictional role models of your childhood. If Lizzie could overcome her stage fright to perform "Hey Now" at the freaking Colosseum, then I think I can come up with a cardboard shelter design in one night. In the end, I pulled out a pretty solid design that I think impressed my professor.

Although the driving force behind my schoolwork was to impress my professors at first, I like to think that it eventually shifted to impressing myself. If you don't feel good about the work that you're producing, then why are you spending time on it at all? I'm not saying you should be in love with everything you create as a designer (because there will probably be a lot of times that the product you design is not intended for you), but you should at least be able to take some pride in it.

When you can see value in what you do, you're going to be more motivated to keep doing it. If you can't, then maybe you should take a step back to think about how you would rather spend your time. Are you spreading yourself too thin? Is there one thing you'd really like to become specialized in or a new skill you'd like to pick up? Whether this leads to a shift in your career, starting a new hobby, or removing something that's causing you stress, we owe it to ourselves to take control of how we manage our time.

Productivity will look different for everyone, whether it's the schedule that works best for them or the environments they prefer to work in. Spending the most time in the studio doesn't make you the hardest worker, and getting projects done quickly doesn't mean you don't care about the work. How we choose to organize our time is no one's business but our own. It's not a tool to prove yourself to your peers or to judge someone else's value.

If spending an extra five hours on a project would make it five percent better, is it worth your time? Should you work to make a career out of a passion of yours, or are you happy keeping it as a hobby? These are things that everyone can decide for themselves. You're allowed to prioritize other things in your life over design or whatever it is you create. Life is full of tradeoffs and sacrifices, but you should be thinking about how your work fits into your life, not how your life fits into your work.

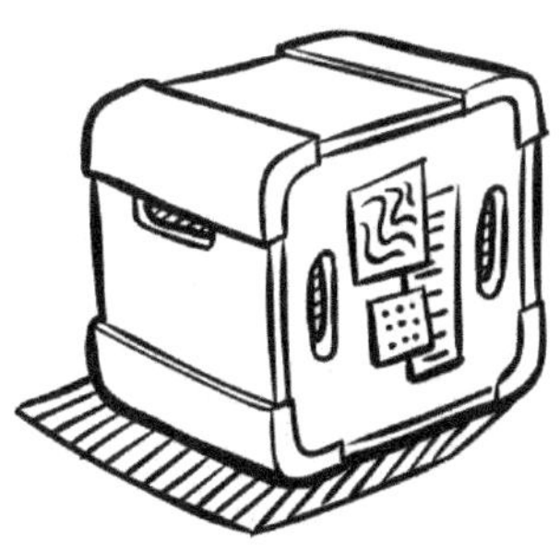

Creative Thinking

When I was growing up, I always thought that being creative and being good at art were the same thing. I think that's because people used to tell me I was both of these. Usually, they would tell me this after seeing a drawing I did of one of my classmates or a painting I did of some flowers. I think what they meant is that I was good at translating what I saw into nice, recognizable images, but that doesn't sound much like a complement to a child. I'm not sure that this meant I was "good at art," since art is subjective, and its value is a combination between technical skills and the meaning a piece holds.

When I was seven years old, painting a picture of some ducks from a photograph torn out of an old calendar, I might have had some skill but I definitely did not have any particular meaning in mind. I just painted some ducks, and didn't think about much at all.

This is what most of my works of art were like when I was younger (although I branched out from ducks a bit). I would make these little re-creations of a landscape or a still life, sometimes taking liberties with colors or scale. Usually, these weren't meaningful statements, just results of, as Bob Ross would call them, "happy little accidents."

I was good at drawing and painting because I did it all the time, but I only did it all the time because I believed I was really good (even when I wasn't). Looking back, I am very grateful for that false sense of confidence that turned a tiny spark of natural talent into an actual skill.

When I was in middle school, one of my favorite pastimes was copying portraits of celebrities in magazines with a mechanical pencil and copy paper. Some were hung with scotch tape on my closet doors, and some were gifted to friends. (My favorite commission was of Sandra Oh for a fellow *Grey's Anatomy* fan.)

Around the time I was starting high school, I got a bit bored of it. The drawings were sort of meditative, and I was proud of myself when they turned out decent, but I felt like I should be doing something more. They were impressive, I guess, but they really weren't all that interesting. They didn't require any thought, just a good sense of awareness, patience, and hand-eye coordination. I started to realize that the fact that they were drawn well did not mean they showed any creativity, and by extension, my skill for drawing did not make me inherently creative.

Although I was still creating something, it felt very limited. I was looking for something to draw just for the sake of drawing, which isn't necessarily a bad thing. I think being creative means using your technical skills, like drawing, to communicate ideas that are new or thought provoking. That's a lot harder than getting Benedict Cumberbatch's eyebrows right.

This realization didn't mean I *wasn't* creative, but the fact that art and creativity were no longer synonymous in my mind really made me question whether or not I *was* creative. If I wasn't the creative one anymore, then who would get to make the PowerPoint for the group project? Being creative was what was expected of me, and it was part of my identity now (my fragile, fourteen-year-old identity).

I felt like a fraud, when in reality, nothing had changed. I was still capable of the work I had been doing that had earned me the creative title in the first place. And it's not like I never did truly creative things. I liked to make videos with my next-door neighbor or sew little crafts, but these things were not art in my mind. They weren't the thing I was supposed to be good at. I had been focusing so much on getting great at the technical side of drawing or painting that I wasn't thinking about the meaning each piece could carry, or how I could be experimenting with them. I suddenly felt very determined to prove how creative I could be, and I wanted to start making things that were totally original.

Needless to say, I was setting myself up for failure. True originality cannot exist because nothing comes from nothing. Everything made has had some influence from what came before it. That's not a bad thing, though. We just have to recognize that inspiration is everywhere, and we couldn't ignore it if we tried. Our experiences influence what we create, so any art is more of a translation of what we already know than something entirely new. If everything worth saying has already been said before, then how might we say something in a new way? Our perceptions are unique, but the content is not. What you decide to bring attention to and how you choose to portray it is where you have creative freedom.

Pursuing originality (or as close as we can get) is a lot less intimidating when you look at it like this. It reminds me of something that had been drilled in my brain from science classes: nothing can be created and nothing can be destroyed; it can only be transformed. (I'm not positive if this was referring to matter or energy or something else, but at least I retained something from those classes.)

"Art is theft." This is a well-known quote from an even more well-known artist: Pablo Picasso. He believed that every artist steals from their environments to fuel their work. Stealing, however, is very different from copying. When you copy something, it is unchanged and, therefore, unauthentic. When you steal something, you make it yours. How can we draw inspiration from something, but transform it so that it becomes our own? Instead of simply recycling stale ideas, we are part of an endless cycle of inspiration, allowing ideas to live on in new ways, reaching new audiences. At least, that's the way I like to look at it.

PSA: I am *not* telling you that it is okay to steal someone else's work and pass it off as your own, and neither is Pablo Picasso. Plagiarism is very bad and just plain mean. The key thing to takeaway here is to "steal" from multiple sources and always give credit where credit is due. Your work can show creativity in the way you combine unlikely things or put a unique spin on something. Otherwise, you're just a copycat, and that's no good.

It sucks to have your work copied, but when you put your work into the world, you have to recognize it as a possibility. I mean, would the alternative of never showing your work to anyone really be better? We have to be willing to risk not getting credit if we want the things we create to be seen by anyone else. Even if our work is stolen or copied, we should at least be happy that it can live on in whatever way it does. (Just like the work we draw inspiration from, and the work *that* work drew inspiration from.)

Isn't that the goal? To put good into the world that will last a lot longer than any of us will? Who cares if we get a pat on the back for it? (Okay, I can admit that I'm not *that* morally mature. I'll take my pats on the back where I can get them, thank you!)

I think that when we feel our work is creative, we can find more fulfilment in it. We can feel proud that we made something new and interesting that nobody else made. This can get a little trickier in design where a lot of our work is collaborative or has stricter restraints. Although, I don't believe you need a blank slate or complete control to be creative. Creativity comes in a lot of different forms, so it's difficult to compare or quantify.

When you go to an art and design school, you're probably going to find some tension between the art majors and the design majors. Each of them feels that they're on the better path, at least a little bit. Designers might think they have a more secure future or are making more practical change in the world. Artists might think the designers are sellouts and their own work is much more interesting, and therefore, they are more creative than designers. While not everyone openly expressed this, there was a certain vibe that we were all aware of.

During the beginning of my freshman year, my school had a designated week called "Majors Week" where we attended presentations for each major before declaring our choice. We had to sign up for at least two presentations, so I went with one of my friends to the interior design studios first. While we were there, an upperclassman asked us if this was our first choice. I said no because I was planning on choosing industrial design. He smiled and said, "I came to this school for ID too, but then I realized I didn't want to spend my whole life designing small parts of a drill no one cares about. I want to design *experiences* for people."

I didn't correct him and say, "Industrial designers create experiences for people, too." I just politely nodded because he was intimidating, and I didn't want to say anything wrong. So, I also didn't say, "ID has a wider reach for creating experiences for people through globally accessible products, but experiencing designed interiors is limited to who can access a certain physical space." And I *definitely* didn't ask, "Who designs all of the products that fill those interior spaces?" (I should mention here that I have a ton of respect and admiration for interior design, I just don't respond well to being patronized.)

I felt that so many people had a very close-minded view of industrial design, and I never understood why. You could design *anything!* Why does your mind automatically go to the most boring things as examples? (Sorry power drill lovers, but yes, I think they are boring.) Even so, those seemingly boring things can be really interesting and fun when you give them a chance. Do you think I was excited about designing a shower head junior year? No, but I ended up having an amazing experience and was really happy with what I made. It even got me my first patent!

When I attended the industrial design presentation for Majors Week, I noticed that the student work examples on display were all of very common, everyday products. No spaceships or latte-making robots, just regular products designed for regular people. I think there were sketches of lawn mowers on the wall, if I remember correctly. I thought this was nice, because it showed me how this program would train students to make real change through things that a lot of people actually use.

During the Q&A that night, one student (with obviously little interest in ID) pointed to the lawn mower sketches and asked, "Do you guys ever do anything creative, or is it all stuff like this?"

Sometimes, I feel like people don't even know what the word creative means. I think it gets confused with things like "expressive." Being creative means being imaginative. It's about being experimental in your thinking or process, not necessarily in the final form a product takes. How it looks is important, of course, but depending on what the product is, a simple or familiar appearance might make the most sense. In the case of industrial design, you are literally creating something to be mass-produced. Because of this, we have to be realistic in how something can be made and how it will be perceived by the end user. If these things aren't considered, then the concept probably isn't worth much.

That being said, we should always be striving for innovation with our designs. How might we make the user's experience better? How might we create additional value? A lot of the time, creative thinking plays more into the problem-solving and functionality of a product rather than its physical style. That's where we can find ways to make someone's life just a little bit easier or more enjoyable. Making it look nice is a valuable part of the process, but there can be so much great design behind those beveled edges. If it's a really good design, then the users probably won't think much about what makes it that way. It just feels intuitive and natural, like it couldn't be designed any other way.

All throughout college, I thought about what my senior cap-stone project would be. I knew it couldn't just look cool, it needed to solve a problem, too. (Bonus points if it solved a problem that people might not realize exists.) I wanted it to be something I cared about, because after all, I would devote months of my life to it.

I decided pretty early on to focus on special education. My

younger sister is autistic, and most of the volunteer work I had done was in the special needs community. I also had an interest in design for education, so it seemed like it would be a good opportunity to explore that. Because I had thought about this project so much, I had a pretty clear idea of what I wanted to do before my last semester even started.

This is a bad habit of mine. I get an idea in my head and get so excited about bringing it to life that I don't always explore every possibility of what it *could* be. It's essential to let yourself be imaginative in those first stages of a design. Sometimes, though, an idea starts to develop and you think, "I just *have* to make this a reality now." I think I did a good job of reeling myself back in to do more research and let that guide my decisions, but being more explorative in the beginning stages is still something I'm working towards.

Our senior projects were a time for us to reflect on who we were as designers, and I came to a surprising realization. I was way more interested in user interaction systems than I was in aesthetic design. I had gotten so excited about what my product would be used for and how it would work that I wasn't even thinking about making it look cool. Then I remembered, *oh yeah, form follows function.* I guess I was doing everything right.

I should probably back up and explain what my project was. I designed a modular storage system that would be used to create sensory spaces. Sensory spaces are areas designed to help kids with sensory processing disorder regulate their sensory input when they are feeling over or under-stimulated. My design was a system of stackable bins with interactive and interchangeable surfaces that provided sensory engagement while reducing clutter. The interactive surfaces could be things with movement, textures, light, sound, etc. The modules were designed to be simple, adaptable, and affordable. Because of this, the product itself was not very exciting-looking. If my sketches of it were hanging on the wall during that presentation freshman year, someone would probably have called it out for not being "creative."

I didn't look at my project as a box I designed, but instead, I looked at it as a system I designed. I mocked up a website where caregivers would take a quiz to determine which interactive surfaces would meet their child's sensory preferences, choose and order their products, then share the space they made on a community page. The box just supported the system. It had rounded corners for safety, nesting features so they could be arranged in different configurations, options for customization, a simple assembly method, and affordable materials.

Every design decision was guided by the service it provided for the user. I showed my creativity in the ways I addressed problems, and I left room for the user to be creative in how they could customize the space that the products were a part of.

So, did Papanek get through to me? Have I come to the realization that designing things to look good is a waste of a designer's time? Not quite. Aesthetic design is still hugely valuable in my eyes, but we should be considering when it makes sense for a product to be heavily stylized and when it makes sense to take a minimal approach. The aesthetic of an object contributes to the overall sensory input it has, so it really depends on the context in which it is used and the practical constraints like cost and materials. Creativity comes at a lot of different stages in the development of a product, not just in the stylization of it.

Although it may come more naturally to some people, I believe that creativity is a skill, not a trait. I think the fact that creativity is so often confused with art discourages a lot of people who might not have traditional artistic skills from ever considering themselves creative. If we're given the encouragement to pursue it, I think all of us have the capability to create amazing things.

I became very intimidated by the pressure that comes with being seen as creative. I can feel confident in working at my technical skills, but what if I just run out of ideas and have nothing new to contribute? It can be scary, especially when we tie our self-worth to the things that we produce. The best tool I've found for dealing with this is to be methodical. (Kind of contradictory, but hear me out.)

Inspiration doesn't come from nowhere, right? Original ideas don't fall out of the sky. If we can find ways to collect ideas to work from, *especially* if we're not sure whether or not they'll actually work, we can begin to build something great. The world is huge and overwhelming. When we create something, we aren't really making something completely new, we're just picking and choosing the parts of our world to steal and transform. Creativity is subtraction. You start with everything, and you narrow that down to what's really valuable to what you're trying to say.

For myself, I often like to do a brain dump of words. I start with one small idea and write down whatever else comes to mind. Once I have a list, I can start to organize what I feel is most important and explore them each individually. I also like to collect images that are compelling to me in some way, categorizing them and analyzing what about them is similar.

Another tool I think is interesting is to take an existing design or work of art and translate it to another genre. Choose an architect and design a clock that reflects their work. Take a song and paint something it reminds you of. I use these methods for all sorts of things: designing, painting, interior decorating, writing, you name it. Finding that starting point is the hardest part, but developing a system that works for you can make it so much less overwhelming to create something.

I encourage you to be creative in different areas of your life. Find a new hobby, makeover your bedroom, develop a new skill. Odds are, your experiences in one area will benefit your work in another. Especially if your job is demanding creatively, give yourself room to play outside of constraints. Be a little selfish sometimes! When it feels like we're constantly producing things to go out in the world, allow yourself to make something for nobody but yourself. It can be such a relief to find escape from the pressure to impress others.

Overall, my best advice for being creative is to have humility. Remember that not everything you do will be great, and be willing to fail. Otherwise, your work will always be limited to what you feel is safe. Taking the safe route can be good too, but it's worth it to at least give the things you're unsure of a shot. They might end up great, and worst-case scenario, you learn something from it. Separate your ego and accept how little you actually know. This shouldn't be scary; it should be exciting! There is so much out there to learn from or to be inspired by, and so many things yet to be created.

Sponsored Studio

Have I mentioned that I have a problem with needing validation from others, or has it just been self-evident? I mean, really. So far, I've talked about seeking praise for my work, upholding my reputation of being the "creative" one, and questioning my self-worth.

I think I've always struggled with self-confidence, and I'm almost constantly worried that I might be doing something wrong. Although, and maybe other creatives can relate to this, that worry seems to go away while I'm designing or making art. Not completely, of course. I will still critique and question the things I've made, but when I'm in the process of actually creating, there's this great feeling of not getting in my own head—a feeling I wish I could carry with me all the time. Because of this, I tend to be much more confident in my work than I am in myself. Pitch my concept to a client? *Sure, that's my job!* Introduce myself to someone at a networking event? *Um, no, that's okay, I'm sure I would just be bothering them.*

I can be really good at hiding behind my work, which will only get me so far. Speaking up for yourself and promoting your own work isn't always easy, but what if you had an excuse to? Imagine if someone else started the conversation and just pointed at you and said, "Hey everyone, this chick did something cool!" (or something like that). Then, maybe you'd feel okay bragging a little. And where can we find these perfect little wing-men for upping our professional game? Competitions and awards.

If you win something, it's like you've been given permission to talk about your work. (Kind of a destructive way to look at it, but also kind of true.) You're not just some boring designer, rambling on about something no one cares about. You're one of those *prestigious* designers now, and *everyone* is very interested in your award-winning designs. (The new title comes with a better parking space and everything.) In reality, your design was just as good before it won an award. The new sticker of approval might have just made you believe it.

Whether or not winning an award changes the value of your work, there's no denying that it makes you feel good. Maybe it's nice to feel like your hard work is recognized, or maybe you see it as confirmation that you're on the right path. I never considered myself a very competitive person, but I think I get a little high from the confidence boost that comes with someone telling me I did something great. It's not about comparing my work to someone else's—it's about my work alone and the value someone (who knows their shit) sees in it. Well, I say that, but what they see in my work probably wouldn't mean much if they saw the same thing in everyone else's. So, maybe I'm more competitive than I thought.

I know it's not a good habit to care too much about what other people think of you, but should the same be said for your work? If successful industry professionals think your work is good, then that must mean you're doing something right. If they have negative feedback, they probably have a very good reason, so shouldn't you try to learn from it?

When you're a young designer, you know so little. Competitions and sponsored projects can be great learning opportunities to evaluate your skills and work on the areas that need improvement. If at the first sign of criticism you shut down and say, "they just didn't get it," you're only getting in your own way. If someone doesn't "get" your design, then you failed at communicating it properly. Products that are designed well should be easily understood. That's just as important as the product looking good or working well.

I think the key takeaway here is to care about what *the right people* think about your work. If your college roommate isn't a big fan of your nursing home bed concept, who cares? It's not designed for them. You should be focusing on the needs and preferences of your user demographic. You're never going to please everybody, so why put so much value in the opinions of people who won't be using the product anyway?

The exception here is the opinions of other designers. They understand that there are guidelines and styles that different products should follow, and they know how to design for different user groups. When they're critiquing your work, they're not telling you what they personally like or dislike (if they're good at giving critiques, that is). They are telling you what they believe will work well or not for the context of your product, and there is a lot of value in that. I mean, what's the point of designing things if they aren't going to be successful? If they don't make someone's life at least a tiny bit better?

My school gave us a lot of opportunities to get this kind of feedback. We had sponsored projects where *real* designers from *real* companies would help us develop concepts that they might actually use! These projects were very exciting because we didn't feel like students during them. We were doing actual design work with formal presentations and everything. We had our skills put to the test and got to understand what it would be like when we would (hopefully) start working as professional designers.

Our first sponsored project was designing shower heads. It might have sounded kind of lame at first, but we were all just thankful the company didn't choose its toilet line. I actually gained a much greater appreciation for shower design after the whole thing. They contribute to a very intimate and personal experience. Some people love taking showers, but when I narrowed in on "caregiver" personas (people who care for someone with a disability, parents of young children, and even dog owners), I found a lot of pain points that I hadn't realized before, and this meant opportunities for innovation.

I won't go into too many details here, but to give you an idea, my concept focused on accessibility and security. The form language of my design was so simple (because, again, the form followed the function), but the brand we were designing for was very sleek and minimal, so it made sense. It also took way less time for me to model and prototype, which was an added bonus.

I worked hard to make my presentation as simple as possible, too. I cut out anything that wasn't necessary to my story, and used graphics in a clever way to highlight features as I spoke. After all twenty-eight students in my class presented to the entire professional design team, we left them alone to decide on the winning projects.

After a bit of stressful small talk amongst ourselves, we were all called back into the classroom to hear their decisions. I felt like I did a really good job, but I had no idea what they thought. My professors seemed like they were impressed with my design work, but that was, like, three people. This was the first time my design skills were being judged by people that didn't know me on a first name basis, and there were ten of them!

As their final presentation began, I was thinking about my project, and what the odds were that they would call my name. Then, I heard my name. I panicked for a second and thought *wait, they really said that, right? I wasn't just thinking really loudly? Well, shit, I hope they did, I'm already standing up.*

Thankfully, I was not making a fool of myself, I actually had won first place. (Well, technically they awarded two more first place awards and three more for second place, but leaving out those details makes me sound more impressive on my resume.)

I guess that settled it. This meant that I was on the right path, and I was doing a good job. I don't think I won because I had the best design. (How do you define "best" anyway when there are so many different directions and factors?) I think I won because my project was very realistic for this specific brand. Having good ideas and refined skills is so important, but so is knowing how to apply them in different scenarios. My design added something new, but it wasn't too out-there.

I was also very thoughtful about how I spent my time, making sure I never bit off more than I could chew. Playing it safe had paid off this time. It had also gotten me my first patent. I can now officially call myself an "inventor," which makes me feel like the dad from *Rugrats*. (I'm not sure if that's a good or bad thing.)

Needless to say, this whole experience was a huge confidence-booster. It was a really great feeling that I didn't want to let go of, so I started taking other competitions really seriously. I kept a list of accomplishments in the Notes app on my phone, and I wanted to grow it as much as I could. I didn't see it as an unhealthy obsession (although there's a small chance that's exactly what it was), I just took full advantage of any opportunities I had. (Except for the one sponsored project where my team didn't place. Those hand saws would never see the light of day again if it was up to me.)

I was happy that I was finding success, but maybe I was putting too much value into winning. I think I started to see it as proof. Proof that I had made the right decisions, proof that my college tuition was well spent, proof that I was *good*. Was that a bad thing? It encouraged me to do better work and make the most of my education. Why did my thinking behind it matter?

What I will say is that I started putting a lot of pressure on myself. I like to think I always had it under control, though. When one assignment of my senior year was a submission to an international student design competition, I knew my chances of placing were slim. So, I wasn't thinking about impressing the judges, I just designed something that I thought was a good idea and would fill some gaps in my portfolio. My project was inspired by something I personally experienced. I know that I said you shouldn't be designing for yourself all the time, but in this case, I stumbled on a real problem that I thought needed some attention.

A few months earlier, my dog had a back injury that would require a lot of rehab. She was the sweetest little wiener dog that had been with me for the majority of my life. I would chase her around my subdivision when she slipped away to go after a squirrel, and now she couldn't even move her back legs. (I'm sorry, I know you didn't sign up for a sad dog story, but it gets happier, I promise.) Throughout her rehab, we had to help her go to the bathroom with a DIY sling and keep her still as much as possible. She wasn't a big fan of her crate, so we would fill a bin with blankets to keep her close to us, but also to keep her safe and secure.

I thought about how so many dogs have to go on crate rest, so why do all the crates suck for this? There are those metal ones that make it really hard to lift your dog out and are too heavy to move around the house with you (in case they don't like being alone). Then, there are the travel ones that can be hard to clean and are so visually closed off. So, I set out to design a crate that kept your dog comfortable and accessible. It had a few other functions that would help your dog in later stages of recovery: a sling to help them walk and walls to block off stairs for preventing another injury. I was really proud of it.

My dog was fully recovered and happily squirrel-chasing again by the time I designed it, but she did a great job modeling for the product photos. I felt really good about how my project booklet turned out, but when I submitted it to the competition, I tried not to get my hopes up. I reminded myself that even if I didn't win, there was still a lot of value in what I made. Not just for my portfolio, but for myself. It was sort of a therapeutic experience. Maybe something good could come from a really hard situation.

And it did. I got the call about a month later that my project had placed third! This wasn't just a "yay, congrats, add it to the resume" kind of competition. It was for a huge trade show in downtown Chicago where I would present my project and talk to the press. (Wow, I used the phrase "the press," I must have made it!) The woman on the phone literally told me, "This call changes people's lives."

I spent a lot of time preparing, buying a new dress for the

award gala (yes, a *gala*) and submitting bios and photos for "the press" while also practicing how *not* to cry when I talk about my adorable dog's very sad injury. I was never able to get very good at networking, but here was my chance. Apparently, past winners even found people to partner with for patenting and selling their product. My experience may be able to help other dog owners have an easier time going through rehab processes. (I had to practice not crying when I thought about that, too.)

Then, something happened. Or, rather, *nothing* happened. The trade show was scheduled for spring of 2020, and a world-wide pandemic wasn't exactly a good time for tens of thousands of people around the globe to have a get-together. So, it quickly turned into a "yay, congrats, add it to the resume" kind of competition. The dress I bought for the gala is hanging in my closet with the tags on as I write this. I was really disappointed, but I had to remind myself that it didn't take anything away from the fact that I won. I had just lost an opportunity, it happens—and often in far worse situations than mine.

My biggest disappointment wasn't that I couldn't post an Instagram looking amazing in that dress, holding my award to let everyone know just how much I had "made it" (but that definitely crossed my mind). I was more disappointed that my design didn't have a chance to become a reality anymore. I mean, I guess it still does. I just have no idea how to do that on my own. I wanted to be able to hand it off and have it magically become a real thing that could help real people (and more importantly, real *dogs*).

So hey, if anyone reading this wants to make this happen, feel free to reach out to me. (Surprise! This whole book is just an elaborate marketing scheme to sell my dog crate invention! Just kidding ... unless?)

So, it wasn't the "life-changing" experience I was promised. What matters is that I designed something really great, and I was recognized for it. It's fine that I didn't get to celebrate the way I wanted. I mean, I was bummed, believe me, but it's fine. Designing should be a selfless practice at its core. No one owes you a round of applause. Your reward comes in the form of whatever positivity your work brings to the world, and that should be enough. (Well, that and money, because you deserve to be paid for your work.)

Designing is a job. Getting recognized or celebrated is nice, but it shouldn't be your main motivation. You have to be okay with not getting credit for everything you do. Not in the terms of someone else stealing credit, I just mean that most people don't care who designed most things. I don't know who designed my bedside lamp, but I still appreciate it. It's just the right size, and the lampshade perfectly matches my macramé wall hanging. I don't know who designed that, either. I mean, I made it, but I bought a DIY kit and followed a pattern that I found online. I appreciated how simple the instructions were and the natural touch of the twig instead of a dowel at the top.

If you do feel like showing your appreciation for well-designed products, there is something you can do that's really easy: write reviews! A lot of the time, people think to write reviews for products if they have a reason to complain, but you can write them when you're happy with something, too. Some designers will actually find their product online to see what people think of it. Learning from criticism is good, but it's also nice to know which things are working well and why. It helps support designers' work by giving it more exposure, and it doesn't cost you a penny to do! Just something to keep in mind.

Recognition of their talents or appreciation of their work

are not the only things a designer can find in competitions. There is also pride. It feels good to know that your work means something to someone.

I felt proud of the work I did while I was in school, but I wanted to know that this pride was deserved. When I toured my college as a high school senior, the industrial design office was covered in posters, all in the same format. Each poster had a small headshot in the top corner, a different year in the header, and the rest was filled with design work. The people smiling out of their windows in the corners were all of the MIAD Student Merit Award Finalists over the years. Leaving the tour that day a lot closer to making my decision, my mom turned to me and said, "Maybe you'll be up there on a poster one day!"

And so, that became the goal. I was going to have my poster, and that was how I would know that I made the most of design school.

The Industrial Designers Society of America (or IDSA) Student Merit Award competition was optional to participate in, but it was never a question for me. After a round of portfolio presentations, one finalist would be chosen from each school to go up against other schools' finalists and be named one of the five district winners. Usually, this is done with verbal presentations at district conferences, but that was no longer happening the year I entered. I knew this, and I was still eager to compete. I didn't care about the exposure; I just wanted the title. (Remember what I said about not seeing myself as competitive? Um ...)

Anyway, I presented my body of work over video chat (again, this is 2020) to a panel of judges and patiently watched my classmates' presentations with my microphone on mute. I'm not an amazing presenter by any means, and I really had no idea how my work would come across to the judges.

The classmates of mine that chose to participate all had really great presentations, and at every other slide, I kept thinking *the judges are going to love that!* I had already poured myself a glass of "at least I tried" Sauvignon Blanc . A few hours after the presentations finished, I got the email that I was the finalist. *Wow , okay.* A goal over four years in the making ceremoniously achieved in an email. It felt sort of weird to celebrate, but another glass of wine seemed justified.

Now, it was time to compete for the district title. *Oh, right, that was the whole point of this.* I wasn't competing against many people, so my chances weren't *that* slim, but these were the best of the best. I wasn't a big fish in a small pond anymore. Although, I guess the pond was still small. Maybe now it was more like I was one of ten really nice lobsters in a fancy restaurant. Like, hey, glad to be here, but those other nine lobsters look really good, I totally wouldn't blame you for picking one of them. (Well, I wouldn't think the lobsters would be very glad to be there, but you get it.)

Still, I imagined what it would be like to win. It's a pretty big deal, and it's a good sign that the winner would have a really successful career ahead of them. People will be expecting great things. Suddenly, it turned from an exciting thing to a scary thing. If I won, that meant that I must be really, really good at design. I would owe it to, I don't know, the *world* to make design a huge part of my life. Isn't that what I wanted? Wasn't that what I was working toward?

I think I started to feel trapped. What if I didn't want to devote my whole life to design? What if I woke up one day and decided I want to climb frozen waterfalls instead? Would I feel like I'm not allowed, like I have the ability to make actual change in the world, and it would be selfish to not devote myself to it entirely?

This spiral went on silently for a few weeks, until I found out that I didn't win. I wasn't disappointed this time; I was actually a little relieved. I appreciated the freedom of not being chosen, still swimming in the lobster tank. (Is this analogy still working?)

I was definitely being dramatic, and I was possibly talking myself into not wanting to win anyway because I didn't think I would. Still, maybe there was a little truth to my thoughts. Of course you're allowed to stop designing (even if you're really, really good). You are in charge of your own life, and what you feel like you owe to others should be determined by *you*. There may have been pressure around the award, but only because I gave it that power.

Competitions can be really great. They can give us confidence and lead to other opportunities, but we should not rely on them as if they're giving us permission to be proud of our work. They are not proof that you are good at what you do, and the judges you're working to impress are not all-knowing. Competitions are just ways to encourage good work and give a little well-deserved recognition to support their communities.

Self-worth comes from following the expectations we set for ourselves. Don't put yours in the hands of someone who doesn't even know you. Impress yourself first, and try not to let the pressure from others get to you. (Most of it's in your head, anyway.)

Professional Practice

Sometimes, I really miss being in school. I'm probably not supposed to admit that, but it's true. There was something so comforting about the structure. I had some freedom in how I scheduled my classes, there was always a clear checklist of what needed to be done, and the grades my professors gave me let me know how I was doing. I was being guided along a path, and I didn't have to stop too long to think about what I needed to be doing. It was always laid out so neatly in my mind (and in my planner). I was constantly working towards something concrete, and everything just seemed easier.

Wait a minute, no. It wasn't easy! I was almost constantly busy with schoolwork, and when I wasn't, there was a looming feeling over my head that I *should* be. I guess it was nice to have clear goals to work towards, but it was draining to always be working towards them. It was also difficult to really be present when I was always looking forward to finishing the next thing. Why do I look back on my experience at school with rose colored glasses? Why do I conveniently forget so many parts that were stressful, annoying, and exhausting?

I think I have a bad habit of idealizing things. I guess there are a lot worse habits to have because it means I have really nice memories of my past and get excited when I think about my future. The problem, though, is when it gets in the way of my ability to appreciate my present. I shouldn't be daydreaming about my blissful time in college (which is far from its reality), I should just be grateful for where it got me.

It can be a scary thing to leave something comfortable, but it's important to have faith that what you've gained from the experience has prepared you for what else is ahead. If you never left, you would never get the chance to put that knowledge to work and see the value that it brought you.

Maybe I have rose colored glasses for my college experience now because I'm in a really good place, so it must have all been good to lead up to this. I have to remind myself that those stressful times *did* exist, but they were necessary for me to walk away with something I could be proud of. That applies to today, too. Things are really good, and I'm grateful, but I tend to let myself get bogged down in stressful things, giving them way more power than they deserve. When something is difficult or scary, I try to see it as something that's leading to a future that will be genuinely worth something to me.

But how can we be sure? How do we know that our hard work will pay off? How do we know that our work is *good* work, or if we're just hopeless and wasting our time? I guess it all really comes down to having trust in yourself and your abilities. (That's vague, I know, so let's try to break it down.)

It's hard to find trust without any reasons (or, feedback) to back it up. Feedback on your skills is so helpful, but remember to take the source of it into consideration. Your professor with decades of experience probably knows what they're talking about, whereas a freshman might need a grain of salt (or two) taken with their advice. (That doesn't mean it doesn't have any value, though!)

Basically, positive feedback from people who are experienced and knowledgeable in this field is a pretty good sign that you're on the right track. Another good sign is when you feel your skills are comparable to your peers. I know that it's hard to judge your own work when you're obviously biased, but try to analyze it in the most basic and objective ways you can. Is your sense of perspective realistic? Are the trends you're following relevant to the user? Is your presentation easily understood? (For this last one, get some other eyes on it, because obviously it will make sense to *you*.)

And, of course, there are competitions and awards. I know that I said not to put too much value on them, especially when it comes to your self-worth (and I stand by that), but they are a good tool for assessing your skills, technical or otherwise. There's not much to lose by entering, so why not? You don't have to win everything you enter for your skills to be acceptable, but if you happen to get some well-deserved recognition, it could do a lot for your self-confidence. (One of my proudest accomplishments is winning the Blue Lake Fine Arts Camp's "Outstanding Camper" award in 2011, which my older sister interpreted as "Star Nerd." Someone has to keep me in check, I guess.)

So, these are all things that can help you build trust in your skills, but what about trust in yourself? That can be a little trickier. What if you have an amazing portfolio, but you just don't have the right personality or mindset to work well as a designer? Is there anything you can do to improve that, or are you just screwed?

During my junior year, I spent a lot of time applying to internships. My portfolio was ready to go, my cover letter template was made, and my resume was polished. All I had to do was plug away at any job posting I could find online. I started early and cast my net wide, so there wasn't too much pressure (yet). When the first couple phone interviews were scheduled, I was feeling good. I told myself that even if they didn't work out, they were great practice. (Although, of course, I secretly hoped that each one would end in the interviewer deciding to hire me on the spot. A girl can dream!)

One of these phone interviews was with a large medical company. (Pop quiz: what kind of products did I say I wanted to design as a freshman? Hint: it rhymes with ... why does nothing rhyme with medical?) Anyway, I was excited about this one. After preparing with my older sister who knows all the insider-lingo of the corporate world, like STAR format questions, I felt ready. The interview went pretty well, and the next step was for me to take a personality quiz. As a proud INFP and Enneagram Type 9, I thought this would be right up my alley.

The "quiz" was done over the phone, and it was more stressful than I had anticipated. Aside from the awkward instances like, "sorry, no, you finish ... oh, okay, um ..." I had to verbalize all of my answers instead of taking my time to decide what box to check. I can't remember if it was supposed to be a "yes or no" quiz, but I think a lot of my answers ended up being "I guess" or "I don't think so." (So, what did *that* say about my personality?)

A few days later, I got the email that my quiz results did not align with what they were looking for in this position, and I would be removed from further consideration. However, I interpreted this as reading, "You are not cut out to be a designer," which sent me spiraling a bit. I started to focus on my flaws. I am not the most social or outgoing by any means, I have a hard time making decisions, and I'm too sensitive. (So please don't leave a bad review of this, or I might cry. Just kidding ... maybe.) Would these things hold me back from being a good designer? And is there any hope of these things changing, or are they just part of who I am?

I think we are all capable of change to some extent, but that doesn't mean we *should* change for something like a job. I appreciated that this company had defined what they were looking for in their future employees. If I had gotten the internship based on my portfolio alone, I might have not been a good fit with their team. (That doesn't mean my design work wouldn't be good for them, but both of these things matter.) There are so many designers in the world, all with different personalities. Some will function better in specific work environments than others, but that doesn't make anyone better or worse at what they do.

Diversity is hugely important in design. Design needs to be for everyone, so it can't all be done by one type of person. Although we can learn to be empathetic when doing work for people that are different than us in some way, the perspective of someone who can relate to a specific group of people is hugely valuable (whether that's based on age, gender, race, sexuality, physical limitations, or something else). Normally, if you stand out in a group, it can be easy to feel self-conscious or left out, but on a design team, being different actually gives you power. You can offer a perspective that no one else can, and that makes you more valuable, not less.

In college, I was the smallest person in my class, which I was often insecure about. I had trouble working with large materials or machinery in the 3D lab, and I even struggled to pin up drawings for critique. (The cork board went really high up the wall.)

During a handle redesign project, everyone in the class measured their hands. To no surprise to anyone, mine were the smallest. This meant that everyone in the class should ask me and the person with the largest hands to test out their models. If we both thought it was comfortable, it would probably be comfortable for everyone with hand sizes between ours. It felt good to be valued for something I was insecure about, and I really embraced it. In my presentation, I even had photos of me struggling to carry a weighted suitcase upstairs with both hands wrapped tightly around my handle. (What I lacked in upper body strength, I made up for with design insights.)

This continued throughout college. I gave user insight quotes for classmates' research, modeled for a photo lifting a chair prototype designed to be extra light, and I proudly brought my own step stool to the studio.

Now that I'm out of school, I'm in a similar scenario. I'm still small, but I'm also the only woman on my design team. This is pretty common because it's still a male-dominated field. Sometimes I feel a bit self-conscious about it, but I just have to remind myself that I'm bringing something unique to the table. Obviously, I want my talent as a designer to be seen as more than being the "girl designer" on the team, but that doesn't mean I should neglect the things that give my work a distinct perspective.

Despite all of this, I still experience self-doubt and sometimes feel like I'm not qualified to be where I am, commonly known as imposter syndrome. This is so incredibly normal, and some of the most successful people admit to feeling this way. It's often described as feeling like it's only a matter of time before everyone else finds you out, like you've been tricking everyone into thinking you're more capable than you actually are.

So, let's humor this. If you can't give yourself credit, then give it to the people around you: *What makes you think you're even capable of tricking them if you're so unqualified? If everyone around you is so smart, then they must have good judgement in trusting you to do your job.* We get so wrapped up in our own heads that we forget everyone else is doing the same thing: being more judgmental of themselves than they are of you.

When you are so worried about failing, you project that fear to those around you (as if they're the ones that this doubt is coming from), but we are our own worst critics. Maybe this comes from setting incredibly high standards for ourselves. Or, maybe it's from not setting any standards at all. If we don't have an image of what success looks like to us, then there's no goal to achieve and, therefore, it's always unattainable. It's important to define what success looks like to you and give yourself credit for the areas where you are meeting those expectations. This should be different for everyone. It doesn't have to be crazy specific, either. For example, the standard for success I've set for myself lately is "business mouse."

When I was younger, there was this clip that would play in between shows on Nick Jr. It was a cartoon of the main characters, Moose and Zee, waiting at the bus stop. They were teaching the viewers what it meant to be taller or shorter. Moose asked, "Who is taller: Zee or the business mouse?" And there was this cute, little cartoon mouse in a suit carrying her tiny briefcase and coffee. (Zee was taller, by the way.)

My mom and I would point out the business mouse every time she came on. For some reason, I dug up this memory recently and decided that I wanted to be like her. I'm not entirely sure what that means. The business mouse just gave off this aura of self-assurance and purposefulness, even though she's just a little mouse. So, now, if I'm out shopping and I find a nice blazer, I'll say to myself *this looks very "business mouse,"* or if I'm attending a design conference, I'll walk in thinking *how incredibly "business mouse" of me.* It's silly, but it makes sense to me, and that's all that matters. (I don't know how I expect anyone to take me seriously after sharing this.)

I know that I should probably have more concrete career goals for myself, but I'm still working through what those might be. For now, I'm just working towards being proud of the work I do and trying my best to be a bit more present. Maybe I don't need a big end goal in front of me just yet, and I can just take small steps, making a new path as I go. Success can be scary, faced with more responsibilities and more chances to fail, but if it wasn't scary, then it wouldn't be so rewarding. Focusing on doing a good job with what's in front of you can make it a lot more manageable to push forward toward bigger achievements.

If the things we're working on don't make us uncomfortable (at least a little bit), then we probably won't grow from them much. Maybe that's okay, depending on your personal goals. It's just important to realize that feeling like you're in over your head doesn't mean you're doing something wrong or you don't deserve to be there. No one expects you to have all the answers, and it's more than okay to seek out help when you need it.

Putting yourself out there (like, oh I don't know, writing a book) can be a very vulnerable experience. There's something really positive in that because you'll learn so much about yourself and gain confidence for the next thing you want to achieve. We should be working to normalize the feelings of self-doubt that we all have in order for us to encourage others to not let it hold them back from what they want to do with their lives.

When I started college, I felt that being a designer is what I was meant to do. Maybe I felt this way because I liked it and people told me I would be good at it. Does that really mean that it's what I was *meant* to do? How can anyone really know that? And if we are all *meant* to do something, is that something allowed to change?

Feelings of pressure or guilt surround the world of design and the type of work that you choose to do within it. There are so many ways you can bring value to the world, both inside and outside the box of "designer" that you're put into. What you do with your life is so much more than the job you have. Realizing the potential each of us have can be a really difficult thing, but once we see it, we should not feel limited in what we are encouraged to do with it. We should consider every possibility and feel empowered by our ability to choose our own ever-growing and ever-changing paths.

As long as we recognize the responsibility and power we carry with every project, however small, we can continue to affect positive change in ways that are meaningful to us. When we are proud of the work we are doing and happy with how it contributes to the rest of our lives and the lives of those around us, we can find fulfillment in designing anything, even a pretty, sexy toaster.

Epilogue

When they ask you to do ten, you give them eleven, right? (Just kidding, literally no one asked for this.)

I wrote this book to work through the different thoughts and feelings I've had, not just on design, but on being a designer. I wanted to reflect on what that meant to me so that I could be more intentional with my work in the future. It's been an interesting and fun journey to get to where I am now, but it's also been scary. (And I have no doubt that it will continue to be scary.) There are so many talented people in the design world doing amazing things, and it's easy to get overwhelmed or second guess yourself.

Believe me, I am no expert. (I probably shouldn't admit that if I expect you to listen to me at all, but it's true.) I have just barely gotten started in my career, but I'm hopeful that I'm starting with my best foot forward.

I might look back at this in the future and think it's silly or naive, and that's okay. We are all constantly growing and changing, and what we believe is allowed to grow and change too. This book is meant to capture a moment in time for myself. What I believe twenty years from now does not take value away from what I believe today. Maybe I'll use this as a way to check in with myself, to be reminded of what's important to me. Or, maybe it will be a benchmark for me to see the progress I have made.

I wrote this for myself, but I hope you could take something positive away from it. When I was struggling with questions of purpose and self-worth, I looked for something to help me make sense of all of it. Maybe this could be that for you.

I think it's important to have conversations with ourselves about what really matters to us and how to be authentic in the work that we do. I also think those conversations can be framed in a lighthearted, approachable way. With so many voices out there telling us what we should care about or what we should be doing with our lives, I hope I could help you hear your own.